STUDENT GUIDE TO ACCOMPANY

The Great Republic

A History of the American People   Second Edition

STUDENT GUIDE TO ACCOMPANY

The
Great Republic

A History of the American People   Second Edition

Bailyn, Davis, Donald, Thomas, Wiebe, Wood

Prepared by
GERALD J. GOODWIN, *University of Houston*

Self-Tests by
Kenneth L. Weatherbie, *Del Mar College*

D. C. HEATH AND COMPANY
Lexington, Massachusetts   Toronto

International Standard Book Number: 0-669-02756-1

Introduction

The purpose of this Student Guide is to help readers use *The Great Republic,* Second Edition, more efficiently and effectively. Like *The Great Republic,* the Student Guide is organized in six parts and thirty-three chapters. For each of the parts, the guide presents a *Thesis* statement and a brief *Chronology* followed by chapters corresponding to those in the appropriate section of *The Great Republic.*

There are a number of possible ways to use this Student Guide. Here is one tested procedure.

First, carefully read *The Great Republic's* introduction to the part that includes the assigned chapter. Then read the Student Guide's *Thesis* statement for that part to make certain you understand the main themes that will be developed in this group of chapters. Use the guide's *Chronology* for that section to establish the sequence of major events during the period. Each time you study a chapter in *The Great Republic,* return to the introduction to that part of the text to note the particular chapter's relationship to the treatment of the whole period.

Second, read *The Historical Problem, The Historical Problem Answered: The Chapter Thesis,* and *The Chain of Arguments and Evidence* for the assigned chapter in the Student Guide. Historians explore the past by asking and answering questions. *The Historical Problem* presents the issues and questions the historian is dealing with in that chapter. *The Historical Problem Answered: The Chapter Thesis* summarizes his or her answers to those questions. Also, *The Chain of Arguments and Evidence* enables you to see more clearly how the historian uses historical evidence to arrive at those answers or conclusions.

Third, read the text of the chapter in *The Great Republic* with the *Student Guide* open to the questions in *The Chain of Arguments and Evidence.* By referring from the text to the Student Guide, a task made easier by the page references in the guide, you will be able to follow the development of the argument and to see more clearly why the historian has drawn the conclusions that form the thesis of the chapter. As you do this, write notes to yourself in the margins of both text and guide so that you can quickly find your way back to the key parts of the chapter. These notes will be particularly useful when reviewing.

Next, read the Student Guide's *People, Places, and Events* section, which will supplement the information and ideas presented in *The Great Republic.*

Now put aside these materials before taking the next step. A break in the study schedule at this point is necessary if the *Self-Test* is to measure accurately your understanding and retention of the material. Take the Self-Test no sooner than the day after reading the assigned chapter or chapters.

Finally, if the completed chapter contains a *Map Exercise* in the Student Guide, work this exercise using the proper map in the back of this guide. The map exercises will strengthen your understanding of the material by making clear the geographical aspects of the historical developments treated in the text.

This suggested procedure may sound tedious and complicated, but in practice it is simple and natural. Many students have found it very effective. It will enable you to understand how historians analyze problems, and it will help you gain a fuller knowledge of the history of the American people.

Contents

PART ONE

Bernard Bailyn *Shaping the Republic*

to 1760

Thesis

The foundations of the American republic were laid long before 1776
in the dreams and enterprises of the adventurers and settlers who tried
to establish traditional social institutions in the New World and in the
societies that resulted from their efforts. The reality of everyday life
in the colonies modified institutions, values, and behavior in ways that
were neither intended nor fully understood. Many colonists were troubled
because their society seemed to deviate in undesirable ways from established and traditional norms. Although American society appeared to be
a familiar variation of the European world on the surface, basic aspects
of life were in fact changed — the character of the family, social relations,
organized religion, economic activity, politics, and government. At first,
most colonists considered these alterations to be detrimental rather than
advantageous. Only later, during the American Revolution, would they
come to believe that these changes had been positive — that their society
represented a simpler, purer, and better order which offered the world
a new social ideal.

   The central theme of America's colonial experience is the development
of a successful but different way of life shaped by peculiar circumstances.

This development was accompanied by the emergence of an idealism out of the eighteenth-century Enlightenment that gave positive meaning to these social changes. The combination of material success and soaring idealism would remain a characteristically American blend. The story of how materialism and idealism originated, and how they were combined, is the indispensable first chapter of American history.

Chronology

1492-1504	Columbus's four voyages to the New World
1607	Founding of Jamestown, first permanent English settlement in North America
1630-1643	The Great Migration of English Puritans
1706	Benjamin Franklin is born in Boston
ca. 1739-ca. 1745	The Great Awakening
1763	Treaty of Paris ends the Seven Years' War

CHAPTER 1

The Background of English Colonization

The Historical Problem

The problem is to explain the features of the British settlements in North America that made them different from other European colonies in the New World. In the area of government, the British colonies were distinguished by the existence of an open and competitive politics quite unlike that of the Spanish-American colonies. How and why did politics and government in British America develop in this distinctive way? Why did a free, competitive politics emerge in the British North American colonies but *not* in Spanish colonial America, though some of the ingredients for its existence were present in the Spanish-American empire?

The Historical Problem Answered: The Chapter Thesis

The origin, settlement, leadership, ideology of colonization, and population of the Spanish empire combined to create a well-organized, hierarchical, bureaucratic structure that blocked the emergence of organized opposition to imperial authority. The English colonization movement sprang from a very different set of circumstances, with different kinds of leaders and settlers, a different ideology of colonization, and different forms of colonial organization. In sharp contrast to Spain, the English crown played a very limited role in overseas enterprise, which sprang rather from the initiative of West-country gentlemen and merchants. The English belief that the nation suffered from the burden of excess population, the availability of capital, and the usefulness of the commercial joint-stock company made England's overseas activities different from Spain's. These same factors prepared the British North American colonies for the emergence and development of a dynamic political society.

The Chain of Arguments and Evidence

Financial Limitations and the "Starving Times"

People, Places, and Events

1. *Adelantados* were granted extraordinary feudal powers in order to enable them to gain control of frontier regions of the Spanish empire. Although they were initially very powerful, the *adelantados* were not able to transmit their authority to a second generation.

2. *The Council of the Indies* was a branch of the royal court which had control of all colonial affairs. The Council was empowered to review and enforce laws, appoint colonial officials, and serve as an appeals court. It exercised its authority in the name of the king, and its power was virtually unlimited.

3. *Creoles* were American-born colonials of Spanish descent. Because so few Spanish emigrated to the colonies, Creoles constituted only a tiny percentage of the colonial population, perhaps only 1.25 percent in the 1570s.

4. *Mestizos* were colonists of mixed European and Indian ancestry. Suffering from a sense of social inferiority, the *mestizos* tended to be politically inert. They formed a lower middle class of farmers and shopkeepers and lacked the experience to express their latent aspirations politically.

5. *Encomiendas* were created by grants of land and of Indian laborers. Potential sources of power capable of competing with imperial authority, the *encomiendas* also produced brutal oppression of the Indians. These institutions were seriously weakened by imperial policy in the early eighteenth century.

6. *Humphrey Gilbert* was an adventurous member of the English gentry and, from his youth, a personal servant of Queen Elizabeth. One of

the first Englishmen to take an active part in overseas ventures, Gilbert received a royal patent in 1578 authorizing him to explore and occupy new lands. Little is known of his first effort in 1578, but in 1583 Gilbert led an English expedition to Newfoundland. On the return voyage, he drowned when his ship foundered near the Azores. He left his dreams and plans to others.

7. *Walter Raleigh,* Humphrey Gilbert's younger half-brother, inherited his colonizing schemes and replaced the unlucky Gilbert as the leader of English colonization activities. Armed with a renewal of Gilbert's patent, Raleigh organized exploratory expeditions and the first attempts at settlement in North America (1585). The first settlement, at Roanoke Island, lasted only for a winter, after which the colonists returned to England. The persistent Raleigh organized another expedition that disappeared, the "Lost Colony" of Roanoke. The dreams and plans of the two vigorous half-brothers inspired other Englishmen who succeeded in establishing settlements a generation later.

8. *The joint-stock company* was formed by investors in order to support a specific, limited enterprise. Joint stocks were designed to be temporary (often for seven years); after the venture was concluded the joint stock and profits were divided among the stockholders. The first successful English colonies were financed through this device.

Self-Test

I. Match each identifying statement with the appropriate name.

a. Humphrey Gilbert (18)
b. Francisco Pizarro (7)
c. Richard Hakluyt (19)
d. Walter Raleigh (20)

e. Francis Drake (18)
f. Hernando Cortés (7)
g. John Cabot (16)
h. Pedro de Valdivia (7)

1. _____ The Spanish *conquistador* who overthrew the Aztec empire and gained control of Mexico.

2. _____ One of the most effective propagandists of English colonization and author of *Discourse of Western Planting.*

3. _____ Explorer who established England's claim to North America.

4. _____ The sponsor of the ill-fated "lost colony" of Roanoke.

5. _____ The illiterate adventurer who conquered the Inca empire of Peru.

Note: Numbers in parentheses indicate page numbers in *The Great Republic* where this individual is identified.

II. Match each identifying statement with one of the items below.

a. Creoles (14) e. viceroy (10)
b. *encomienda* (12) f. planters (24)
c. *cabildo* (11) g. *mestizo* (15)
d. merchants (23) h. joint-stock company (25)

1. _____ The most powerful governmental officer in the Spanish-American empire.

2. _____ The small, but politically ambitious social group in Spanish America whose access to authority was frustrated by the circumstances of their place of birth.

3. _____ The royal arrangement made with private individuals in order to promote colonial settlement in the Spanish empire.

4. _____ The royal arrangement made with private individuals in order to promote colonial settlement in the English empire.

5. _____ The economically ambitious social group that financed England's major colonizing ventures in the early seventeenth century.

III. Match each numbered statement with one of the following.

a. Describes colonization by the Spanish.
b. Describes colonization by the English.
c. Describes colonization by both the Spanish and the English.

1. _____ New World discovery and colonization were actively promoted and controlled by the monarch. (13)

2. _____ Colonization returned immediate and immense wealth. (16)

3. _____ Colonies were viewed as convenient places to relocate religious dissenters and the unemployed. (19)

4. _____ Colonial administration was centralized, hierarchical, and patriarchic. (9)

5. _____ Prior experience indicated that the native population in the colonies would be savage and ungovernable. (24)

Note: Numbers in parentheses indicate page numbers in *The Great Republic* where this item is identified.

Circle the phrase that best completes each statement.

6. English expansionists were initially interested in the intensive colonization of   (a) the English West-country,   (b) Ireland, (c) Newfoundland. (24)

7. The disruption of the wool trade promoted England's expansion by stimulating   (a) a search for new markets,   (b) the conversion of pastures into cropland,   (c) the rapid growth of the gentry class. (17)

8. One characteristic of Queen Elizabeth I that made her accession a stimulus to colonization was her   (a) great wealth,   (b) Protestant faith,   (c) close friendship with the Spanish monarch. (17)

9. The early colonizing ventures of the English in America were primarily intended to   (a) return a quick profit,   (b) extend the crown's territorial holdings,   (c) Christianize the native people of America. (25)

Answers to the Self-Test

  I. 1. f; 2. c; 3. g; 4. d; 5. b
 II. 1. e; 2. a; 3. b; 4. h; 5. d
III. 1. a; 2. a; 3. b; 4. a; 5. b; 6. b; 7. a; 8. b; 9. a

CHAPTER 2

Transplantation

The Historical Problem

The problem is to explain how the establishment of English colonies in North America and the transplantation of Englishmen and English culture to the New World affected the kinds of communities that developed there. Was there a common pattern to the experience of colonization, despite the fact that the planting of these settlements was neither planned nor given common, centralized direction? If there was a common experience, how did this pattern affect early American life?

The Historical Problem Answered: The Chapter Thesis

The various English colonies of the seventeenth century reveal a persistent pattern in spite of diverse motives, founders, and plans. The different colonizing ventures began with great expectations and noble, even utopian, plans. But the reality of social transplantation to a wilderness shattered these plans and produced suffering and frustration. The adjustment to the realities of life in the New World took place gradually. Out of this process there slowly emerged new societies that differed in important ways from the European originals on which they had been based.

The Chain of Arguments and Evidence

Virginia: Squalor, Struggle, and a New Way of Life   TEXT PAGES

1. How was the Virginia Company organized and financed?   31-33
2. What problems did the Jamestown settlers face?   32-33
3. What changes took place in the reorganized company
   and colony after the rechartering in 1609?   33

People, Places, and Events

1. *John Smith* (ca. 1579-1631) was a soldier who had served in European campaigns before he joined the Virginia Company's expedition to Virginia that founded Jamestown. Although he was in the settlement only a short time, from the first landing in 1606 to October 1609, the adventurous and imaginative Smith left his mark on the venture. At a crucial moment in Jamestown's critical early days, Smith provided the energetic leadership that imposed discipline on the demoralized colonists. He also contrived to obtain needed food supplies from the Indians. In addition, Smith explored Chesapeake Bay and left an excellent map of the region.

2. *The "headright" system* was devised by the Virginia Company to encourage settlement. Anyone who transported a settler to Virginia was given fifty acres of land, hence the name: each "head" conferred a "right" to fifty acres. It is important to note that the land was given, not to the individual who actually came, but to the person who transported him or her or who paid for the transportation. The headright system was central to the land policy of Virginia and other southern colonies during the seventeenth century. It is an interesting illustration of colonial promoters' efforts to use the abundant land of the New World to subsidize colonization.

3. *Indentured servants* were persons who signed contracts which bound them to work for a specified period of time, usually four years, in exchange for passage to America as well as food, housing, and clothing during the term of service. People without means and young people getting started found this a convenient way of migrating to the colonies. Indentured servitude made it possible to convert labor into a commodity which could be bought and sold (in the form of the indentured contracts) and shipped across the Atlantic to labor-hungry America. Indentured servitude is not to be confused with slavery; these white servants passed into the free colonial population after their terms of service ended.

4. *William Bradford* (1590-1657) became a Separatist when he was a boy in England and accompanied those Puritan Separatists who migrated to Holland in 1609. One of the leaders of the Pilgrim colony in Plymouth, Bradford succeeded Governor John Carver after the latter's death, and he was elected and reelected governor of Plymouth from 1621 to 1656, with the exception of five years. A man of spiritual strength, prudence, and good judgment, he was a tower of strength in the settlement. His *Of Plymouth Plantation* is an American classic.

5. *John Winthrop* (1588-1649) was a member of the English gentry and a lawyer. A deeply religious man, his commitment to the cause of Puritanism swept him into the Puritan group that planned Massachusetts Bay Colony. A man of considerable ability, Winthrop led the first large group of the Great Migration to New England in 1630. The first governor of Massachusetts Bay, Winthrop was the dominant figure in the Puritan settlement. A model of the Christian magistrate, Winthrop protected community order, articulated group ideals, and managed the practical aspects of the colony's affairs. His *Journal* is a major source for the early history of Massachusetts and New England.

6. *Quakers* were radical offspring of the Puritan movement who were committed to the doctrine of the Inner Light. This religious teaching held that there was a spiritual light or divine spark within each person, which was a source of divine truth. They sometimes called this Inner Light the "Christ within." Their teaching that this divine light could provide religious truths was potentially disruptive, since individuals were supposed to respond to the voice of Christ within them rather than to the outward authority of church or state. For this reason, others considered the Quakers religious fanatics and radicals of the worst sort.

7. *Proprietary grants,* such as those given to the Calverts, the Carolina proprietors, and William Penn, differed from corporate charters in that the proprietary grants conferred authority on an individual or individuals rather than on a corporate group. These proprietary grants also tended to be feudal or manorial in nature. The Maryland grant is a good example of this. There is evidence that the Calverts had researched antique feudal grants in England and modeled the charter on practices that had long been outdated in England. Thus members of the English gentry and landed elite were stimulated by America to dream of manorial estates.

Self-Test

I. Match each identifying statement with the appropriate name.

    a. William Bradford (40)   e. Lord Baltimore (48)
    b. John Colleton (56)   f. Lord De la Warr (34)
    c. Roger Williams (47)   g. John Winthrop (43)
    d. John Smith (33)   h. Anne Hutchinson (45)

1. _____ The Salem minister who, when banished because his religious views threatened the good order of Massachusetts Bay, founded Providence.

2. _____ The founder of Maryland as a refuge for English Catholics, but also as a place where discrimination against Protestants was not permitted.

3. _____ Leader of the Pilgrim settlement that established the small but influential Plymouth Plantation in 1620.

4. _____ The self-disciplined and resolute governor of the Puritan's "city upon a hill" colony in Massachusetts Bay.

5. _____ Romantic adventurer whose forceful leadership kept the early Virginia settlers from starving to death.

II. Match each identifying statement with one of the items below.

a. patroons (53)   e. chattel slavery (37)
b. demesne (50)   f. headright system (35)
c. indentured servitude (37) g. separatism (38)
d. antinomianism (47)   h. proprietors (56)

1. _____ A system of attracting labor to America by granting 50 acres of land to anyone who paid for the transportation of a settler.

2. _____ A system of labor devised to attract workers to America by offering payment of their passage in return for their promise of temporary service.

3. _____ The religious heresy of seventeenth-century New England that threatened the Puritan Church by demanding the direct relationship of the individual with God.

4. _____ A system of labor characterized in America by lifetime, inheritable, and transferable servitude.

5. _____ Those to whom English colonization grants to America were most often made after the Restoration in 1660.

III. Circle the phrase that best completes each statement.

1. Colonial offshoots of Puritan Massachusetts Bay included   (a) Maryland and Delaware,   (b) Plymouth and New York,   (c) Rhode Island and Connecticut. (48)

2. The first colony in which slavery emerged as a form of exploitive labor was   (a) Maryland,   (b) South Carolina,   (c) Virginia. (37)

3. The Dutch West India Company's main interest in founding New Netherlands was   (a) the fur trade,   (b) agriculture,   (c) Christian missionary work among the natives. (51)

4. Unlike the Puritans, Pilgrims were   (a) tolerant of deviant religious views,   (b) Separatists,   (c) interested in eventually returning to England. (38)

5. The successful migration to Pennsylvania was mainly stimulated by (a) forceful advertising,   (b) the growing popularity of Quakerism, (c) Penn's offer of free land to all comers. (62)

6. Virtually all of the first English colonies in America had in common (a) a shared commitment to religious liberty,   (b) friendly relations with the Indians,   (c) the frustration and failure of the original plans of the founders. (31)

Answers to the Self-Test

I. 1. c; 2. e; 3. a; 4. g; 5. d
II. 1. f; 2. c; 3. d; 4. e; 5. h
III. 1. c; 2. c; 3. a; 4. b; 5. a; 6. c

CHAPTER 3

Europe in the Wilderness: American Society in the Seventeenth Century

The Historical Problem

The problem is to understand the common characteristics of the seventeenth-century British-American colonies and to explain the deviations from European life that developed in them. What common features did the diverse colonies exhibit? How did life in the colonies differ from life in England? What produced these differences? Were they the result of conscious purpose or of uncontrolled circumstances? Why did colonists consider many of the differences to be undesirable?

The Historical Problem Answered: The Chapter Thesis

In every aspect of seventeenth-century colonial life — the economy, the family, the social order, and religion — there was change and uncertainty. These changes did not fulfill the visions and plans of colonial founders, and settlers resisted rather than pursued social innovation. Novelty sprang from circumstances that forced reluctant colonists to modify their institutions and ways of behaving. These distinctive features of colonial life had not hardened into new forms by 1700. Colonists viewed these changes with regret because they did not fit the traditional social ideals the settlers had brought with them from England. Hence, the peculiar aspects of colonial social life, economic organization, and religion were lamented as signs of decline.

The Chain of Arguments and Evidence

Population Growth and Structure   TEXT PAGES

   1. How did the process of migration affect the structure
      and composition of the colonial population?   68–70

People, Places, and Events

1. *Maryland's Act Concerning Religion* (1649) imposed the death penalty for blasphemy and for violations of the Sabbath; in effect it banned from the colony anyone who did not believe in the divinity of Christ. But it did provide that all Christians who believed in the Trinity could practice their religion without harassment or interference. This act was a significant departure from the tradition of enforced religious uniformity, but it did not end religious conflict in Maryland.

2. *Establishment of parishes* in Virginia was an effort to duplicate the parishes of England in the New World. The parish was both an ecclesiastical unit and a unit of local government, a practical implementation of church-state ties. The governing body of the parish was the vestry. Vestrymen handled all questions dealing with the financing and support of the parish church, and they also handled such civil problems as relief for the poor and care of orphans. The parish was the smallest organ of local government and a geographical organization of the church.

3. *Congregationalists* were Puritans who believed that each church should consist of those who had received God's saving grace, and that each

of these churches should be autonomous, handling its own affairs in its own way. Thus Congregationalism emphasized that the church should consist of the elect, and that each church should be run by those elect. They could select their minister and control membership in the church.

The Puritans who settled New England were primarily Congregationalists. When they put their ideas into practice, it was necessary to moderate them in certain ways. New England Puritans had to devise methods to limit the autonomy of individual congregations, and they found it necessary to make some adjustments in their procedures for admitting new church members. It was a system of church organization that emphasized decentralization and local control.

4. *"The elect" and "the unregenerate"* were terms used by Puritans to designate the major spiritual categories of their theology. The Puritans were basically Calvinistic and they believed that God had chosen some men and women to spend eternity in heaven. To these chosen few, the elect of God, He sent His saving grace. The unregenerate formed the mass of mankind; trapped in sin, they would spend all eternity in hell. The Puritan ideal was to form churches that would enfold the elect, exclude the unregenerate, but regulate the lives of all in ways that would conform to proper Christian conduct.

5. *The consigment system* was used in the seventeenth century to market the tobacco crops of Maryland and Virginia. English merchants transported and marketed the tobacco; in the meantime, the merchants paid the costs of the process and gave advances to the planters. Having sold the crop, the merchants deducted their charges, marketing costs, and the advances, and credited the remainder to the planters. This system locked the Chesapeake planters into an endless debt cycle and committed them to an inflexible agricultural economy that discouraged diversification of crops and the limitation of production.

Self-Test

I. Match each identifying statement with one of the items below.

a. consignment system (75)
b. primogeniture (82)
c. doctrine of "works" (88)
d. triangular trade (74)
e. predestination (87)
f. sumptuary laws (79)
g. Congregationalism (89)
h. doctrine of the covenant (89)

1. _____ The legal requirement that estates were to be kept intact by allowing their inheritance by eldest sons only.

2. _____ Legal method used to control the extravagant dress and social habits of those in colonial America whose station in life didn't justify their adoption.

3. _____ In the Puritan faith, this required that church members help non-members achieve salvation.

4. _____ In the Puritan faith, this asserted that one's salvation was the unchangeable decision of an omnipotent God.

5. _____ A marketing arrangement whereby southern colonial planters sold their tobacco through English agents who extended them credit.

II. Circle the phrase that best completes each statement.

1. By comparison to the English population, the population of the American colonies was   (a) slow growing,   (b) youthful,   (c) sickly. (69)

2. English immigrants to America generally assumed that their economic life there would be   (a) highly competitive,   (b) narrowly specialized,   (c) closely regulated. (71)

3. The commercial economy of New England was unstable because (a) the Indians refused to cooperate,   (b) the Dutch in New York manipulated the market to their own advantage,   (c) the supply of trade goods was highly unpredictable and unreliable. (73)

4. Seventeenth-century Englishmen generally believed that society should be organized   (a) hierarchically,   (b) democratically,   (c) like a "state of nature". (77)

5. One effect of colonial conditions on traditional family life was to (a) reduce the economic value of children,   (b) discourage marriage,   (c) loosen dependence on family relationships. (80)

6. Major changes in the Church of England in Virginia were made because   (a) few settlers wanted organized religion in the colony,   (b) physical conditions required major innovations of traditional ways,   (c) Indians clamored to join the Church of England. (82–83)

7. Massachusetts Bay Puritans believed that church membership should (a) include all residents of a community,   (b) include only the "saints" who could demonstrate their having been chosen for salvation,   (c) be based solely on one's outward behavior. (89)

8. The higher value among those listed here for the Puritans was (a) self-satisfaction, (b) community welfare, (c) economic acquisition. (90)

Answers to the Self-Test

I. 1. b; 2. f; 3. h; 4. e; 5. a
II. 1. b; 2. b; 3. c; 4. a; 5. c; 6. b; 7. b; 8. b

CHAPTER 4

Elements of Change,
1660–1720

The Historical Problem

The problem is to explain how British efforts to form their colonial settlements into an empire between 1660 and 1720 affected the growth and
development of the American communities. How did these imperial plans
and activities interact with social and economic conditions in the colonies?
What were the consequences of these changes for American society?

The Historical Problem Answered: The Chapter Thesis

British efforts to form the mainland colonies into a more coherent, integrated empire were not completely successful. Imperial authority was
too divided and confused to operate efficiently. On the level of commercial regulation, the empire was somewhat more successful, but even
here the complexity of regulatory legislation bred confusion and inefficiency.

   The use of the patronage system in the appointment of imperial officials
undermined the colonists' assumption that social and political leadership
should be joined. The increase in the number of imperial officers coincided
with the emergence of native colonial aristocracies in New England towns,
on southern plantations, and in the larger port towns. The sudden appearance of these provincial elites in societies whose social structures
were not fully formed produced considerable tension that revealed itself
in the colonial rebellions that exploded from 1676 to 1689. In the meantime, the whole colonial culture was becoming more "provincial," as the
colonies grew while partially separated from the parent culture. The educational departures contrived by New England Puritans to meet the special
needs of their society moved American cultural life in a new direction.

The Chain of Arguments and Evidence

People, Places, and Events

1. *Sir Edmund Andros* (1637-1714) was one of the very few colonial governors who approximated the modern figure of the "professional" colonial civil servant. This was because Andros served in a number of different colonial posts over a period of years. His most important appointment was as "Governor-General of the Dominion of New England."

Although it is doubtful that any administrator could have succeeded in such a post, given the New Englanders' tradition of self-government, Andros's regime was conspicuously unsuccessful. He violated the religious scruples of the Puritans by forcing them to allow Church of England services to be held in a Congregationalist meeting house in Boston. He disturbed the whole basis of society by reexamining all land titles. He limited both the frequency and the functions of town meetings, and he imposed taxes without Assembly approval. These and other policies were more than enough to infuriate people who disliked the imposition of the new government in the first place. When the Glorious Revolution provided the opportunity, New Englanders overthrew the Andros government.

2. *The Dominion of New England* was created in 1686 by King James II to unify all the northern colonies under one government. Massachusetts, Plymouth, Connecticut, Rhode Island, New York, and New Jersey were included. From one point of view, the Dominion was an administrative reform of considerable significance. If it had been successful, it would have counteracted the political fragmentation of the northern colonies. There were serious obstacles to this reform — the difficulty of governing such a vast area, for one — but the Dominion soon disappeared along with its royal creator.

3. *The Acts of Trade and Navigation* were enacted by Parliament to regulate the trade of the empire in accordance with the principles of mercantilism. The major acts were passed in 1660, 1663, and 1696, although there were many other enactments as well. The system was largely established by 1696 and did not change substantially until the 1760s.

   The principal features of these famous navigation acts are simple. First, they provided that all the trade between England and her colonies should take place on English ships; colonial-built vessels were included as English ships. Second, they provided that certain valuable commodities produced in the colonies could only be shipped from the colony of production to another British colony or to England. These were called "enumerated commodities." The most important enumerated commodities were sugar and tobacco; only the latter was grown in mainland North America. The purpose of this provision was to make certain that the empire benefited from the production of desirable goods that were not readily produced in Europe. Third, the navigation acts required that all goods originating in Europe which were being shipped to the colonies must be shipped through England. This was intended to make certain that England derived the maximum benefit from colonial trade. In general, the purpose of the navigation acts was to guarantee that the benefits of empire would not be dissipated by allowing other nations to reap the commercial rewards of British enterprise.

4. *Jacob Leisler* (1649–1691) migrated from Germany to New Netherlands in 1660 as an employee of the Dutch West India Company. A successful merchant and wine importer in New Amsterdam (New York City), he married into an established Dutch family, with whom he quarreled bitterly. When the local militia rose against the New York branch government of the Dominion of New England, Leisler was a militia officer. He quickly rose to the leadership of the insurgents and, after the lieutenant governor fled, claimed to exercise legitimate authority in the province on the basis of a letter from the new king to the absent lieutenant governor.

   Leisler's rule prompted considerable opposition from those in New York who constituted the local establishment. They now claimed that Leisler, who was an "outsider," and his supporters used their power illegally against honest, reputable citizens. Unfortunately for Leisler, this opposition included the wealthiest and potentially most powerful men in New York. When the authority of the home government was reestablished, they got their vengeance, and Leisler was hanged.

5. *The Treaty of Utrecht* (1713) ended the War of Spanish Succession which colonists called, after the monarch, Queen Anne's War. By the treaty, Britain acquired Newfoundland, Nova Scotia, Hudson Bay, and the right to supply slaves to Spanish-American colonies for a thirty-year period. The treaty marked the beginning of a period of peace during which the colonies flourished.

Self-Test

I. Match each identifying statement with the appropriate name.

   a. William Berkeley (110)   e. Jacob Leisler (111)
   b. Charles II (93)   f. Edmund Andros (97)
   c. Nathanial Bacon (110)   g. James II (96)
   d. William Byrd II (114)   h. John Culpeper (111)

1. _____ The monarch who wished to strengthen the British empire's administration of her North American colonies by creating two viceroyalties there.

2. _____ The leader of the Greenspring Faction in seventeenth-century Virginia and its remarkably successful, long-time governor.

3. _____ Leader of a rebellion against the power of the eastern elite in late seventeenth-century colonial Virginia.

4. _____ The rebel leader who temporarily controlled the colony of New York during the disruption that accompanied the Glorious Revolution in England.

5. _____ The British imperial officer who was deposed by an uprising of Massachusetts Puritans during the Glorious Revolution.

II. Match each identifying statement with one of the items below.

a. Navigation Acts (96)
b. Dominion of New England (97)
c. Protestant Association (112)

d. Board of Trade and
   Plantations (94)
e. mercantilism (95)
f. provincialism (113)

1. _____ The central agency of English imperial administration throughout the eighteenth century, although of limited effectiveness.

2. _____ The doctrine employed by the British that justified government regulation of the economy in order to provide for the common welfare.

3. _____ An experiment in administrative consolidation of England's colonies which, however, collapsed during the Glorious Revolution.

4. _____ Created by Parliament to regulate the trade of the American colonies and promote the welfare of the imperial economy.

III. Circle the phrase that best completes each statement.

1. Imperial officers who served in America were generally selected on the basis of   (a) competitive examinations   (b) nomination by colonial legislatures,   (c) the patronage of English political leaders. (98)

2. The main factor explaining the rise of a colonial aristocracy was (a) membership in the English aristocracy,   (b) royal favor, (c) the declining availability of land in the colonies. (100)

3. The new colonial elite was distinguished from the remainder of the colonial population primarily by   (a) education,   (b) wealth, (c) ambition. (106)

4. Bacon's Rebellion in Virginia signaled   (a) the origins of colonial discontent with British rule,   (b) the unstable authority of the colonial aristocracy,   (c) the origins of the militia system for Indian defense. (110)

5. To the founders of New England, education was presumed to be primarily the responsibility of the   (a) church,   (b) family, (c) government. (115)

Answers to the Self-Test

I.   1. g; 2. a; 3. c; 4. e; 5. f
II. 1. d; 2. e; 3. b; 4. a
III. 1. c; 2. c; 3. b; 4. b; 5. b

CHAPTER 5

American Society in the Eighteenth Century

The Historical Problem

The problem is to describe and explain the distinctive features of the American colonies in the eighteenth century. What were the most important characteristics of eighteenth-century American society, economy, religion, and politics? How did the colonies differ from Europe and from their earliest colonial beginnings? What emergent patterns would influence the later development of American society?

The Historical Problem Answered: The Chapter Thesis

Circumstances so changed eighteenth-century American society that it did not fit the traditional assumptions about social organization, economics, religion, and politics. Inherited assumptions held that cultural diversity was undesirable, but colonial America was ethnically and racially pluralistic. A large portion of the population lived in relative comfort, but one-fifth of the Americans were held as chattel slaves. Although land was readily available, a traditional landlord class of security and leisure did not come into existence. And mercantile enterprise remained open even as a merchant aristocracy formed. The revolutionary Great Awakening transformed religious life and accelerated the emergence of America's religious denominationalism. The gap between theory and reality was widest in colonial politics where factional divisions, instability, and conflict made colonial political life very different from that of contemporary England as well as from the ideal of ordered harmony. Eighteenth-century America was torn between inherited values and new social realities.

29

The Chain of Arguments and Evidence

People, Places, and Events

1. *Scotch-Irish* migrants to America came from Northern Ireland where
   Protestants from Scotland had settled. Forced to the New World
   by economic hardship in Ireland, the Scotch-Irish came in great numbers during the eighteenth century. Largely poor and Presbyterian,
   they were usually pushed to the backcountry, or frontier, where
   land was cheap and Indians more plentiful. Tough, intolerant, quarrel-
   some, the Scotch-Irish became early America's preeminent frontiers-
   men. They formed the plain white yeomanry of the southern colonies'
   western portions. Andrew Jackson was descended from settlers such
   as these.

2. *Freehold tenure* was the equivalent of outright ownership of land.
   In seventeenth- and eighteenth-century England there were innu-
   merable varieties of tenure. The abundance of land in the colonies
   made the more restrictive forms of tenure irrelevant and made tenancy
   a temporary rather than a permanent condition.

3. *The formation of the Society for the Propagation of the Gospel in
   Foreign Parts* in 1701 is a monument to English philanthropy. The
   Society (or the SPG) was funded by private donations in England to
   support Church of England ministers and missionary work throughout
   the empire. The Society sent many ministers to serve Anglicans in the
   American colonies; it also supported missionary work among American Indians and slaves. Although it was not particularly efficient,
   the Society contributed significantly to the religious life of American colonists. This pioneer English missionary society is still in existence.

4. *Jonathan Edwards* (1703-1758) was the intellectual leader of New
   England Puritanism during his generation, and he has had a profound
   influence on American Protestantism. A grandson and ministerial
   heir of Solomon Stoddard, Edwards graduated from Yale before
   taking over Stoddard's parish in Northampton, Massachusetts. From
   his pulpit, he preached an intellectually revitalized brand of Calvinism
   that united the religious insights of the original Puritans and the
   psychological insights of eighteenth-century science. A creator and
   defender of the Great Awakening, Edwards became one of the most
   original thinkers in early America.

   Edwards's most significant contribution to religious thought was
   his argument that the affections (emotions) were indispensable to a
   genuine spiritual experience. Thus he legitimized the emotionalism
   that was the center of American revivalism. He was ousted from his
   parish after a dispute with his congregation and became an Indian

missionary in Stockbridge. He died shortly after accepting the first presidency of the College of New Jersey (Princeton).

5. *George Whitefield* (1715-1770) was a Church of England minister and a member of the Oxford "holy club" with the other founders of English Methodism John and Charles Wesley. In England, Whitefield (pronounced Whít-field) inaugurated "field-preaching" out of doors. In the colonies, he traveled from Georgia to the district of Maine, ostensibly to collect funds for an orphanage in Georgia but, most importantly, to preach the revival message.

   More than any other person, Whitefield shaped the revivals into a single movement. One of the great preachers in any century, he delivered a message that had tremendous effect on his audiences. On the surface his preaching was conventionally Calvinistic, but his real spiritual power lay in the call for his hearers to experience the emotional New Birth of conversion or regeneration. A leader of the Calvinistic wing of what became English Methodism, Whitefield always seemed happiest in America. He preached his way through some or all of the colonies in 1739-1741, 1744-1748, 1754-1755, 1763-1764, and 1769-1770. It seems fitting that George Whitefield is buried in Newburyport, Massachusetts, where he died in 1770.

6. *Gilbert Tennent* (1703-1764) was the son of a famous father, William Tennent. The two led Presbyterianism in the middle colonies and cooperated in founding a so-called "Log-College" at Neshaminy, Pennsylvania in 1727. The name is misleading because the school in fact trained ministers in the traditional curriculum and functioned as a sort of theological seminary. A preacher of the Great Awakening in New Jersey, Connecticut, and Massachusetts, Gilbert Tennent's most spectacular contribution to the revivals was his 1740 sermon, *The Danger of an Unconverted Ministry,* which warned against ministers who had not experienced conversion and encouraged lay people to judge the spirituality of their ministers. The result was to reverse the relationship between ministers and the laity, a situation that contributed to the decline of ministerial authority.

7. *New Lights* were those who supported the revivals. Among Congregationalists, the prorevivalists were called New Lights; among Presbyterians, the prorevivalist group was called New Side.

8. *Old Lights* were those who opposed the revivals. Among Congregationalists, antirevivalists were called Old Lights; among Presbyterians, the antirevivalist group was called Old Side. The names reveal the splintering consequences of the Great Awakening for institutional religion.

9. *The Glorious Revolution* (1688-1689) was one of the most important constitutional crises in English history. In order to protect the Protestant succession to the British throne, King James II was forced into exile and in his place William and Mary reigned in the name of Protestantism. These changes involved a significant increase in the power of Parliament, and so the Glorious Revolution marked a major turning point in the journey toward constitutional monarchy.

Self-Test

I. Match each identifying statement with the appropriate names.

    a. Gilbert Tennent (139)   d. Devereux Jarratt (139)
    b. Robert Walpole (122)   e. George Whitefield (138)
    c. Jonathan Edwards (138)   f. Thomas Bray (137)

1. _____ The Church of England minister who was a founder and early leader of the Society for the Propagation of the Gospel in Foreign Parts, perhaps the most vital organ of the Church of England in the American colonies.

2. _____ The brilliant English preacher who loosed the floodgates of evangelicalism during an astonishingly effective revivalist tour of America.

3. _____ A grandson of an eminent New England religious leader, he provoked some of the first stirrings of what came to be the Great Awakening in America.

4. _____ The Scotch-Irish Presbyterian proponent of an "experimental" religion among the evangelical "New Light" communities of southern New England.

II. Match each identifying statement with one of the items below.

    a. factionalism (143)   e. halfway covenant (136)
    b. Saybrook Platform (136)   f. freehold tenure (128)
    c. balanced government (141)   g. denominationalism (135)
    d. factors (131)

1. _____ These replaced the old consignment system for marketing tobacco by locating in the southern backcountry and buying tobacco outright from small planters.

2. _____ A consequence of the splintering of church affiliations during the Great Awakening, it produced the naming of several new Protestant sects.

3. _____ The measure adopted by New England Puritan ministers to address the growing crisis in church membership and the decline of the faith's inner fervor.

4. _____ A condition of colonial politics that produced a remarkable level of conflict and disputation between many and diverse narrow-interest groups.

III. Circle the phrase that best completes each statement.

1. The two main groups of European immigrants in the eighteenth century were the   (a) Irish and German,   (b) English and Irish, (c) Scotch-Irish and German. (123)

2. In the eighteenth century, the most rebellious slaves were those who (a) were most assimilated into white society,   (b) were newly brought from Africa,   (c) had been brought to the colonies from the West Indies. (127)

3. In the American colonies, land ownership was   (a) widespread in the form of freehold tenure,   (b) widespread in the form of tenancy,   (c) restricted to a relatively small number of landlords. (128)

4. The general standard of living in the colonies was   (a) generally higher than in Europe,   (b) about the same as in Europe, (c) lower than in Europe. (132-133)

5. The Great Awakening was in part   (a) a result of the fact that the colonies were isolated culturally,   (b) a reaction to the spiritual lethargy that infected the colonial churches,   (c) a result of greater institutional unity among colonial churches. (135)

6. The political assumptions of the American colonists included the conviction that   (a) democracy was the best form of government, (b) the English constitution was seriously defective,   (c) the British government ideally balanced monarchy, aristocracy, and democracy. (141)

7. Colonial politics differed from English politics of the same period in all of the following ways *except*   (a) there was wider popular participation in colonial politics,   (b) colonial governors had more patronage at their disposal,   (c) colonial politics was less stable and more factional. (143-144)

Answers to the Self-Test

I. 1. f; 2. e; 3. c; 4. a
II. 1. d; 2. g; 3. e; 4. a
III. 1. c; 2. a; 3. a; 4. a; 5. b; 6. c; 7. b

CHAPTER 6

The Enlightenment's New World

The Historical Problem

The problem is to determine whether the surface joy with which Americans greeted the accession of George III and the British victory in the Seven Years' War accurately reflected the full range of Anglo-American relations in the middle of the eighteenth century. Were there subsurface tensions between the colonies and England? What were the causes of both latent and overt conflict between the two?

The Historical Problem Answered: The Chapter Thesis

As the reign of George III began, the future of the American people seemed promising, but there were serious strains in the relationship between the colonies and Britain. The intercolonial wars, that ended with the French and Indian War, generated friction between the colonies and the Mother Country. The home government's efforts to maintain the mercantilist system increased the points of conflict. At the same time, Americans became increasingly more self-conscious of their own separate identity as a simple, rustic, innocent people. Although they assumed that their future lay in the British empire, the buried antagonism was real. The consequences of these strains and conflicts would depend on how the complex problems of the Anglo-American world were managed.

The Chain of Arguments and Evidence

"Rule Britannia"   TEXT PAGES

1. How did the imperial wars of the eighteenth century gen-
    erate antagonism between the colonists and Great Britain?   150–156

The Alienation of the State

The American

People, Places, and Events

1. *William Shirley* (1694-1771) was an English lawyer who practiced law in Boston before he succeeded in having himself appointed royal

governor of Massachusetts. An able politician, Shirley's governorship was generally successful. During the intercolonial wars, Governor Shirley found himself involved in military affairs for which he had neither the experience nor the capacity. It was Shirley who organized and planned the 1745 campaign against Louisbourg. This venture was famous in New England forever after. Of the achievement, it has been written that the campaign "had a lawyer [Shirley] for contriver, a merchant [William Pepperell] for general, and farmers, fishermen, and mechanics for soldiers." During the French and Indian War, Shirley actually took command of a British army in the field following General Braddock's death. This adventure was much less successful.

2. *William Pitt* (1708-1778) became principal secretary of state in the spring of 1757 in the ministry formed by the Duke of Newcastle. Pitt replaced older military commanders with younger and more active men. He moved from a defensive to an offensive strategy and determined to drive the French from North America; Pitt engaged Frederick of Prussia to keep France distracted on the Continent, while in America, he tried to cut off the flow of illegal trade from English to French colonies. His coordinated approach to military planning and command led the way to British victory.

3. *The Treaty of Paris* (1763) ended the Seven Years' War. By the treaty, England acquired Canada, the Floridas, and some islands in the West Indies. Cuba was returned to Spain, as were the Philippines. The treaty ended France's power in North America, but not French culture which the British now had to incorporate into their empire.

4. *The Iron Act of 1750* was passed by Parliament to adjust the mercantile system to the reality of increased iron production in America. Iron manufacturing had become one of the largest industrial enterprises in the colonies. The Iron Act was designed to discourage the production of finished iron products in the colonies while allowing colonists to export bar and pig iron to England.

5. *The Currency Act of 1751* was limited in application to the New England colonies. It prevented them from making paper money full legal tender. Existing paper was to be retired as scheduled in the original legislation. Limitations were placed on the issuance of bills to pay government expenses.

6. *Benjamin Franklin* (1706-1790) was born in Boston where he was brought up as a child of pious Puritan parents. He soon grew away from the explicit religious teachings of his Puritan heritage, but he never threw off the discipline that was part of that way of life. As a youth, he moved to Philadelphia, a town which was on the verge of

becoming the cultural center of the American world. From this time on, Franklin's name and Philadelphia were inseparably linked.

As soon as his printing and publishing enterprises provided sufficient income, Franklin devoted himself to the many interests and activities that captured the intellectual energy of Enlightened thinkers in Europe and America. Franklin's contributions to the study of electricity were original and startling enough in his generation to win him the title "the Newton of electricity." Many of his other experimental activities were deceptive in their simplicity but added to man's knowledge. His interest in practical gadgets, lightning rods and stoves for example, reflects the Enlightenment's interest in improving the condition of mankind.

Franklin was not religious by conventional standards; he represented a new figure, one who based virtue on its own utility rather than on supernatural sanctions. In many ways, Franklin's life was similar to that of his Puritan ancestors; he stressed the importance of hard work, self-denial, and moral discipline. But he no longer believed in the God of the Puritans, and he did not share their ardor for spiritual expression.

Map Exercise

Pitt's Strategy in the French and Indian War

Review the text's discussion of Pitt's strategy to break the French arc of control north and west of the British colonies. Refer to the map on page 153 of the text.

1. On the map on p. 271 at the back of this Student Guide, indicate the following:

   a. Identify:

Quebec	Lake Champlain
Louisbourg	St. Lawrence River
Boston	Fort Duquesne
Albany	Fort Niagara
Montreal	Fort Ontario
Lake Ontario	Fort Frontenac

   b. With arrows of one color, indicate the lines of attack that led to the first British victories of 1758 in the west, the south, and the east which began to break the "iron ring" of French control.

   c. With arrows of a different color, indicate the second phase of the British strategy of 1759 which was successful in defeating the French in Canada.

Self-Test

I. Match each identifying statement with the appropriate name.

   a. Benjamin Franklin (165)   d. William Pitt (154)
   b. James Wolfe (155)   e. George Washington (155)
   c. Jeffrey Amherst (155)   f. Edward Braddock (154)

1. _____ Led a British military expedition against the French at Ft.
   Duquesne at the onset of the French and Indian War which
   ended in disaster.

2. _____ The British politician who directed British military affairs
   with decisive and effective leadership during the French
   and Indian War.

3. _____ The one American who seemed to represent the uniqueness
   of American society to Europeans.

4. _____ The British general who lead his troops in a brilliant assault
   on the Plains of Abraham against the French at Quebec
   during the French and Indian War.

II. Circle the phrase that best completes each statement.

1. Unlike other colonial wars, the French and Indian War   (a) involved
   North America as a central theater of operations,   (b) required the
   use of American colonial troops,   (c) involved troops from the
   regular British army. (153)

2. The French and Indian War had all of the following results *except*
   (a) England gained control of Canada and Florida,   (b) the British
   national debt was enormously increased,   (c) the regulation of
   imperial commerce was relaxed. (156)

3. The major effect of the Molasses Act of 1733 was to   (a) cause
   considerable illegality as smuggling and bribery spread,   (b) cut off
   colonial trade with foreign sugar islands,   (c) ignite the first serious
   American questioning of Parliament's authority over the colonies.
   (158)

4. British policy toward manufacturing in the colonies was based on the
   assumption that   (a) manufacturing should be confined to England,
   (b) the colonies should manufacture certain products while England
   manufactured others, but that colonial products could not be ex-
   ported,   (c) the British government should encourage and subsidize
   manufacturing in the colonies to supplement English industry. (158)

5. Colonists devised various "paper money" schemes because (a) they wished to avoid making payments to English merchants, (b) the English pound sterling fluctuated in value, (c) the colonies lacked an adequate supply of gold and silver coins. (159)

6. A description of the developing American self-image in the eighteenth century would *not* include the word (a) innocent, (b) unsophisticated, (c) democratic. (162)

7. From the point of view of Enlightened Europeans, the Pennsylvania Quakers were (a) religious fanatics, (b) the embodiment of American virtue, (c) skillful politicians who knew how to use power wisely to achieve their ends. (162)

8. European environmentalists believed that the special character of Americans was largely shaped by (a) the material conditions of the North American continent, (b) human nature, (c) their European heritage. (162)

Answers to the Self-Test

I. 1. f; 2. d; 3. a; 4. b
II. 1. a; 2. c; 3. a; 4. a; 5. c; 6. c; 7. b; 8. a

PART TWO

Gordon S. Wood *Framing the Republic*

1760–1820

Thesis

The American Revolution is the most important event in American history:
it not only created the United States, but it defined the highest ideals
of the American people. The Revolutionary experience made it possible
for diverse Americans to think of themselves as a single people, a people
with a special destiny to foster liberty in the world. The ultimate origins
of the American Revolution can be found in the gradual changes in the
colonists' inherited institutions and ways of behaving that had been taking
place since the seventeenth century.

The immediate origins of the Revolution lay in the colonists' resistance
to the extension of British imperial authority in the 1760s. The Revolution justified the society that had come into existence in the colonies,
and it continued the transformation of American society that had long
been under way. By the early nineteenth century, the forces released
in the Revolution had brought a new kind of society into existence. By
1815 and the end of a second war against Great Britain, the republic was
secure, and the Revolution was completed.

Chronology

1765	Stamp Act enacted by Parliament
1775	Battles of Lexington and Concord; Second Continental Congress
1776	Declaration of Independence
1783	Treaty of Paris ends War for American Independence
1787	Constitutional Convention drafts new federal Constitution
1797–1801	Second Great Awakening
1800	Republican Revolution of 1800
1803	Louisiana Purchase
1815	Treaty of Ghent ends War of 1812

CHAPTER 7

Sources of the Revolution

The Historical Problem

The historical problem is to understand the connection between British efforts to reorganize the empire in the 1760s and the origins of the American Revolution. Why did British authorities decide to reform the empire? What measures did they adopt? Why did Americans resist these imperial reforms? How did they oppose those measures? How did the crisis in imperial relations influence colonial political life?

The Historical Problem Answered: The Chapter Thesis

A host of problems required that the British empire be reorganized in the 1760s. Besides the imperial expansion that resulted from the Seven Years' War, there were also pressures from population growth and territorial expansion within the colonies that increased conflict between settlers and Indians and among backcountry whites. The expanding imperial economy raised the colonial standard of living and increased colonial indebtedness to British merchants. Imperial reform was undertaken at a time when political confusion was increasing because of instabilities within British politics, and when the wartime economic boom in the American colonies had collapsed. Colonists reacted vigorously and violently to imperial reorganization, and resistance to the Stamp Act united Americans politically as never before. By the end of the 1760s, the imperial reorganization program had ignited a crisis of major proportions. The Tea Act and Coercive Acts pushed the colonists into open rebellion. The Continental Congress's adoption of the Continental Association signalled the emergence of a new political order in America. As these events unfolded, the imperial controversy became entangled with the

45

local politics of the various colonies. A new kind of more popular politics emerged as an unintended consequence of the imperial crisis. British attempts to reorganize the empire precipitated the American Revolution.

The Chain of Arguments and Evidence

People, Places, and Events

1. *Samuel Adams* (1722-1803) was the central figure in the development of an opposition movement in Massachusetts. Adams was graduated from Harvard College in 1740 and then joined his father's brewery business. But his true passion was politics. A member of the Massachusetts legislature from 1765 to 1774, Adams developed a base of political strength in the town of Boston. He took the lead in stimulating popular opposition to the Sugar Act, Stamp Act, and Townshend duties. He also encouraged the agitation that climaxed in the Boston Massacre. An organizer of the Sons of Liberty, Adams helped to establish the Boston Committee of Correspondence in 1772 and supported the creation of a network of similar groups throughout the colonies.

   Perhaps Adams's main contribution to the Revolutionary movement was his continued agitation of the imperial question during the period of relative calm after the repeal of the Townshend duties in 1770. He seems to have been one of the first Americans to come to the conclusion that only independence would solve the political problems of the colonies. In the climactic days of the opposition movement, Adams helped to organize the Boston Tea Party and, as a delegate to the Continental Congress, he helped to propel the colonists toward the Declaration of Independence. After the Revolution (from 1793 to 1797), he served as governor of Massachusetts. Always fearful of central power, he initially opposed the Constitution of 1787.

2. *Thomas Hutchinson* (1711-1780) was Samual Adams's bitter political enemy in Massachusetts. This Harvard graduate served in the Massachusetts legislature where he was Speaker of the House for two years before being defeated for reelection. He was then appointed to the governor's council as well as to a judgeship. Hutchinson was appointed lieutenant governor in 1758 and chief justice of Massachusetts in 1760. His public life exemplified one of the characteristics of eighteenth-century politics, the practice of plural officeholding by which one individual held a variety of (usually appointive) posts in the executive and judiciary of a colonial government at the same time.

Hutchinson's support for the controversial British measures that were provoking colonial opposition made him very unpopular, but he was appointed royal governor of Massachusetts in 1771. During his tenure, some of his letters to British ministers were obtained by Benjamin Franklin and published in America by Samuel Adams. The letters supposedly demonstrated that unwise advice from colonial officials like Hutchinson was partly to blame for the obnoxious British measures. Their publication provoked a storm of objection, and the Massachusetts House petitioned the king for Hutchinson's removal. In 1775, General Gage replaced Hutchinson who went to England to defend his troubled administration. He died there five years later.

3. *Patrick Henry* (1736-1799) was a Virginia storekeeper and farmer who began to practice law in 1760 and became a successful and well-known attorney. Perhaps his most famous early case was the "Parson's Cause," during which Henry argued that the royal disallowance (veto) of a Virginia law had violated the compact between ruler and ruled and that, as a result, the king had forfeited the right to the obedience of Virginians. This was more theoretically dazzling than practical, but it helped put Henry in the most advanced group of Virginians who opposed the British government's reorganization of the empire.

As a member of the House of Burgesses in 1765, he criticized the Stamp Act and introduced seven resolutions, one of which asserted that only the General Assembly of Virginia had the power to tax

Virginians. The House of Burgesses adopted some of the resolutions, but rejected the most fiery. The publication of all seven in colonial papers added to Henry's standing as the most radical opposition leader in the Old Dominion. When the royal governor dissolved the Virginia Assembly, Henry led an extralegal meeting of the Burgesses and called for a continental congress.

He was declared an outlaw by proclamation of Governor Dunmore in May 1775, but he got his political revenge by becoming governor of Virginia from 1776 to 1779 and again from 1784 to 1786. He opposed the Constitution of 1787 out of fear of a consolidated central government and declined George Washington's offers, in 1795, of the offices of secretary of state and chief justice. His last political act was to win a seat as a Federalist delegate to the Virginia legislature.

4. *The Stamp Act* (March 1765) required that revenue stamps be affixed to most documents. Violators could be prosecuted in vice-admiralty courts which did not have juries. The purpose of the act was to raise revenue which the home government intended to use to pay the costs of maintaining an army in America. Parliament hoped to raise £60,000 per year; with other revenues it was expected that about one-third of the estimated £400,000 to maintain the army could be raised in America. In order not to offend colonial sensibilities, the ministry appointed Americans to be stamp agents. Authorities on both sides of the Atlantic were surprised by the unanimity and vigor of the popular outrage. Even many Americans who later became loyalists thought that the Stamp Act was an unwise measure.

5. *The First Continental Congress* (September–October 1774) met in response to the Coercive Acts. It was crucial in creating a unified opposition movement. The Congress claimed that only colonial assemblies could properly legislate for the colonies, subject only to the king's veto. The meeting also declared the Coercive Acts unconstitutional and adopted the Continental Association for enforcing the economic embargoes against Britain.

Map Exercise

North America in 1763

Review the text discussion of the disposition of land in North America among European powers in 1763.

1. In 1763, a number of European nations occupied territory in North America. On the map on p. 272 of this Student Guide, using different colors, shade in and label the areas belonging to: England, Spain, and Russia.

2. The Proclamation Line of 1763 was an attempt by the British government to keep the colonists from expanding westward. (a) Show its position on the map. (b) Indicate areas reserved for the Indians.

Self-Test

I. Match each identifying statement with the appropriate item below.

a. Quebec Act (187)   e. Stamp Act (188)
b. Sugar Act (187)   f. Tea Act (196)
c. Declaratory Act (190)   g. Townshend duties (191)
d. Proclamation of 1763 (187) h. Quartering Act (192)

1. _____ The 1767 regulatory taxes imposed on colonial imports of glass, lead, paint, paper, and tea that reignited American resistance to British authority.

2. _____ Also known as the American Revenue Act, it provoked the first deliberately organized colonial protest.

3. _____ Wrongly identified by Americans as part of the hated Coercive Acts, this extended the boundaries of Canada to the Ohio River, thus threatening the territorial claims of several colonies.

4. _____ Intended to rescue the financially troubled East India Company, the passage of this act in 1773 ended a period of relative peace in the imperial crisis.

5. _____ The first direct tax on the colonies, this act exclusively and explicitly intended to raise revenue.

II. Circle the phrase that best completes each statement.

1. Colonial population growth and expansion between 1763 and 1776 encouraged (a) social unity, (b) political tranquility, (c) economic commercialization. (176-184)

2. A new element in British imperial policy following the French and Indian War was the decision to (a) maintain a standing army in North America, (b) place Indian policy in the hands of the colonists themselves, (c) use taxes on imports as a way to regulate colonial trade. (185)

3. One of the factors encouraging the expansion of colonial settlement after 1763 was (a) the removal of Indians to the West, (b) the removal of the French threat by the British victory in the French

and Indian War, (c) the encouragement given to the westward movement by the British government. (185)

4. As a politician, King George III was (a) full of good intentions but inexperienced, (b) one of the most skillful in the eighteenth century, (c) a malicious and dangerous tyrant. (185)

5. Throughout the imperial crisis during the 1760s, Americans argued that (a) Parliament could levy external but not internal taxes, (b) Parliament could levy no taxes, whether internal or external, (c) the British government had no legal authority whatsoever over the colonies. (193)

6. The Stamp Act was finally repealed because (a) colonial petitions convinced the British government that the measure was unconstitutional, (b) the Grenville ministry simply changed its mind about how best to raise revenue in America, (c) popular violence in the colonies and pressure from English merchants convinced Parliament that it was unwise. (190)

7. The British measure that sparked open rebellion in America was the (a) Stamp Act, (b) Tea Act, (c) Coercive Acts. (196)

8. The colonists did agree in 1774 that Parliament, from necessity, (a) could regulate the trade of the empire, (b) had the right to disallow (veto) colonial legislation, (c) could define the rights of Englishmen. (197)

9. The oratory and writing of Patrick Henry and Thomas Paine advocated the mobilization of a popular political movement based on (a) the knowledge of constitutional rights, (b) feeling, (c) the availability of experienced leadership. (199)

Answers to the Self-Test

I. 1. g; 2. b; 3. a; 4. f; 5. e
II. 1. c; 2. a; 3. b; 4. a; 5. b; 6. c; 7. c; 8. a; 9. b

CHAPTER 8

The Revolution: Ideology and War

The Historical Problem

This chapter is concerned with the need to explain the surprising vehemence of the American rebellion and to understand how the American Revolution developed its overpowering historical significance. The trade acts and tax levies did not seem to justify the rebellion. How then are we to explain the Revolution? And on what grounds did Americans justify their rebellion? How did the political debates over imperial policy affect American political thinking? How did the imperial crisis affect colonial political behavior? What explains American success in the War for American Independence? What were the origins and significance of the political ideology of republicanism?

The Historical Problem Answered: The Chapter Thesis

It was not the specific enactments of the British government that explain the sudden American uprising; it was the meaning that Americans attached to those actions. The colonists tried to understand the purposes of the British government and their own rights in relation to it. Their conclusions were shaped by the political ideology of the country Whigs. Under the influence of these country-Whig political ideas, Americans interpreted British measures as a conspiracy against liberty. In the imperial debates, the colonists denied that Parliament could tax them, and they rejected the idea of virtual representation in Parliament. British insistence on unitary sovereignty led logically to American independence. When war broke out, Great Britain had no chance of winning because it was involved in a revolutionary struggle that enjoyed widespread popular support. During this struggle, Americans increasingly identified their cause with the radical political ideology of republicanism which offered a new social ideal based on virtue and equality. During the Revolution, Americans came to think of their society as a special asylum for political liberty and of their United States as the hope of a republican future.

The Chain of Arguments and Evidence

Republicanism

People, Places, and Events

1. *John Dickinson* (1732-1808) was a Pennsylvanian who helped in
   spire organized intercolonial opposition to the parliamentary measures
   that provoked colonial rebellion. Dickinson was the main author
   of the "Declaration of Rights and Grievances" adopted by the Stamp
   Act Congress. His influential *Letters from a Farmer in Pennsylvania*
   were first published as fourteen essays in the *Pennsylvania Chronicle*
   from November 5, 1767 to January 1768, and later as a pamphlet.
   In this widely reprinted work, the Pennsylvanian argued that although
   Parliament could regulate trade, it did not have the authority to tax
   colonists. He declared the Townshend duties unconstitutional.

   Dickinson composed the Olive Branch Petition adopted by the
   Continental Congress in July 1775. This petition begged the king to
   prevent further armed conflict until a reconciliation could be arranged. He helped to compose the "Declaration of the Causes and
   Necessity of Taking Up Arms" which the Congress also issued. This
   defense of the American position did not yet advocate independence.
   The busy Dickinson also headed the committee that drafted the
   Articles of Confederation under which the United States was governed

until the adoption of the Constitution of 1787. He was instrumental in leading the way toward the new national government.

2. *The Declaratory Act* was adopted by Parliament on March 18, 1766, the same day on which Parliament repealed the Stamp Act. Americans paid little attention to this act in their understandable excitement over the repeal of the despised Stamp Act. The Declaratory Act stated that Parliament had complete authority to make laws binding on the American colonies "in all cases whatsoever." It was an unequivocal assertion of theoretical sovereignty.

3. *Richard Henry Lee* (1732-1794), a member of the Virginia elite, became an ally of Patrick Henry while a member of Virginia's Assembly. Lee worked with Patrick Henry and Thomas Jefferson in proposing a system of intercolonial correspondence. A delegate from Virginia to the First Continental Congress, he was an early supporter of American independence. Appropriately it was Lee who introduced Virginia's resolution of independence which, when passed by Congress, actually severed the political connections between the colonies and Britain. Later Lee served as president of Congress. He opposed adoption of the Constitution of 1787 on the ground that it did not have a Bill of Rights. Some of his proposals were incorporated in the first Ten Amendments to the Constitution. He served as United States senator from Virginia from 1789 until his retirement in 1792.

4. *The Second Continental Congress* met in Philadelphia beginning on May 10, 1775, while the shots fired at Lexington and Concord were still ringing in the air. Thomas Jefferson was now a delegate from Virginia, and several of the notable conservatives from the First Continental Congress were absent. Congress took responsibility for the troops that had gathered around Boston in the aftermath of Lexington and Concord. It was this Congress that led the movement toward independence after the Olive Branch Petition (July 1775) and other efforts toward reconciliation failed. Congress was the central government legitimized by the Articles of Confederation. It led the colonies and states until the adoption of the Constitution of 1787.

5. *Thomas Paine* (1737-1809) came to the attention of Benjamin Franklin when Franklin was a colonial agent in England. Encouraged by Franklin, Paine migrated to America in 1774 where he plunged into the movement of opposition to British policies. His famous pamphlet *Common Sense* was published anonymously early in 1776. In it Paine ridiculed the monarchy and mobilized public sentiment to support independence. *Common Sense* is reputed to have sold a total of 500,000 copies, an astonishing total for the day. After

brief army service, Paine held minor clerkships in congressional government and in Pennsylvania.

In 1787, Paine went to France where he wrote in defense of the early phases of the French Revolution and held up the republican side of a classic political argument with Edmund Burke. As political fortunes in revolutionary France shifted, Paine found himself imprisoned. Fortunately, the American minister to France, James Monroe, secured his release.

Back in the United States, Paine published his *Age of Reason* which criticized orthodox, organized Christianity from a deistic point of view. The aging radical now found himself unpopular in the republic he had helped to found. He died in poverty and neglect.

6. *The Declaration of Independence* was approved on July 4, 1776 by twelve colonies (New York's delegates joined them later). The Declaration, largely the work of Thomas Jefferson, announced and justified the decision for independence. The justification of independence begins with an admirably clear and concise summary of the principles of government as worked out by England's John Locke. These principles included the idea that men create governments to achieve certain ends. Among the ends of government is the protection of the natural rights which all men have. When a particular government became destructive of the very end for which it existed, Jefferson argued according to Locke, it was the "Right of the People" to change the government. The bulk of the Declaration is devoted to proving that the situation of the colonies now met these conditions — that is, that events demonstrated that King George III was attempting to establish absolute tyranny over America.

7. *The Treaty of Paris* (1783) ended the War for American Independence. Of the five American commissioners, three — John Adams, Benjamin Franklin, and John Jay — handled the negotiations. Great Britain recognized American independence and agreed to boundaries that extended American sovereignty to the Mississippi River in the West, the Great Lakes in the North, and to Spanish Florida in the South. Other articles provided for joint navigation of the Mississippi River by Great Britain and the United States and for removal of the states' legal impediments to the collection of pre-Revolutionary British debts. Congress was required to urge the restoration of seized loyalist property. The boundaries reconized in the treaty were extremely advantageous to the United States. Conflict between Britain and the United States over the implementation of treaty provisions soured Anglo-American relations in the following years.

Map Exercise

British Strategy in the Revolutionary War

Review the text's discussion of the battles of the Revolution and the accompanying text maps on pp. 212, 216, and 219.

1. On the map on p. 273 at the back of this Student Guide, locate and identify the following places:

Boston	Philadelphia
Lexington/Concord	Saratoga
New York City	Yorktown
Cowpens	Princeton
Charleston	Savannah
Trenton	Wilmington, North Carolina

2. Draw arrows of different colors to indicate the location and extent of major British campaigns in the following years:

   a. 1774-1775
   b. 1776-1777
   c. 1778-1781

3. Why did the geographical focus of British campaigns shift during each of the three periods mentioned above? What was the significant change in strategy after 1778?

Self-Test

I. Match each identifying statement with the appropriate name.

a. John Dickinson (208)	e. Edmund Burke (207)
b. Thomas Jefferson (223)	f. John Burgoyne (217)
c. John Adams (221)	g. Henry Clinton (218)
d. Thomas Hutchinson (209)	h. Nathanael Greene (218)

1. _____ The author of the persuasive and influential *Letters from a Pennsylvania Farmer* who denied that Parliament could levy taxes of any kind on the colonies.

2. _____ The British commander whose surrender at Saratoga in 1777 was the major military turning point of the American Revolutionary War.

3. _____ The remarkably skillful American commander whose army chased the British across the Carolinas and into Virginia before the victory at Yorktown in 1783.

4. _____ One of three American diplomats who negotiated the Treaty of Paris in 1783 that ended the American Revolutionary War and gained the colonies their independence from Britain.

5. _____ The most eloquent proponent of the idea that independent farmers were "the chosen people of God" and hence the ideal citizens of a republic.

II. Match each identifying statement with one of the items below.

a. actual representation (206)
b. sovereignty (208)
c. Tories (203)
d. virtue (223)
e. country-opposition ideology (204)

f. virtual representation (206)
g. paternalism (222)
h. republicanism (222-223)
i. Whigs (203)

1. _____ The colonists' argument that they could only be taxed by persons known and chosen by themselves who represented them in their own legislatures.

2. _____ The argument, expressed especially well in the Declaratory Act, that every political state could have only one single and supreme undivided locus of authority.

3. _____ The argument that England had become corrupted and conspired to destroy the liberties of colonial Englishmen; it helped justify colonial resistance to British policies before 1776.

4. _____ The social and political ideal of America's Revolutionary leaders that envisioned a society ruled by men of merit and inhabited by equally independent citizens living in harmony.

5. _____ The English political term attached to those colonists who were "Loyalists," that is, those who refused to chose independence from the British empire for America.

III. Circle the phrase that best completes each statement.

1. Perhaps the major influence on the colonial leaders' understanding of their conflict with Britain was   (a) the Bible, along with the political works of John Calvin,   (b) the economic pressure of an expanding population,   (c) the political criticism of England written by radical Whigs. (204)

2. The Declaration of Independence places the responsibility for America's grievances on   (a) King George III,   (b) Parliament,   (c) Loyalists. (211)

3. As the Ameircan Revolutionary War began, Americans had the advantage of   (a) a well-trained professional army,   (b) a vast and rugged territory to defend,   (c) a newly-constructed and well-equipped navy. (213)

4. A major problem that England had to contend with during the American Revolutionary War was   (a) a shortage of well-trained military officers,   (b) communications and logistics across the Atlantic Ocean,   (c) overestimating the strength of the rebel armies. (213)

5. In the American Revolution, ideology was   (a) unimportant,   (b) based upon the Puritan heritage of most colonists,   (c) summed up in the view of an ideal republic. (222)

Answers to the Self-Test

I. 1. a; 2. f; 3. h; 4. c; 5. b
II. 1. a; 2. b; 3. e; 4. h; 5. c
III. 1. c; 2. a; 3. b; 4. b; 5. c

CHAPTER 9

The States and the Confederation

The Historical Problem

The problem is to explain how the Revolutionary experience shaped the republican state governments, and how it influenced America's republican society. What features did the first state constitutions exhibit? How did these frames of government reflect the imperial debate and Revolutionary events? What kind of central government did they establish? What were the social and economic consequences of the Revolution? Why did Americans revise their state governments in the late 1770s and early 1780s?

The Historical Problem Answered: The Chapter Thesis

The state constitutions of 1776-1777 gave formal political expression to the lessons Americans had learned during the colonial period and the Revolutionary crisis. The first state constitutions weakened the power of executives in order to protect against future tyrannies. The central government under the Articles of Confederation reflected Americans' fear of centralized authority. The Revolution and the War for Independence accelerated some social and economic changes that had long been underway, and they introduced some new forces. These social and economic developments further weakened traditional forms of social organization. The optimism of Revolutionary republicanism also stimulated cultural enterprises, influenced family structure, and produced an antislavery movement. The Revolution and the influence of republicanism accelerated the establishment of an egalitarian social atmosphere and increased the number of different interest groups. These changed conditions convinced some Revolutionary leaders that the state governments established in

60

1776 and 1777 had to be altered in order to protect American society from the despotism of popular legislatures. This wave of constitutional revision strengthened executives, upper houses, and judiciaries at the expense of popularly-elected lower houses of legislatures. The theoretical support for such changes was provided by the idea that a constitution is fundamental law immune from legislative tampering.

The Chain of Arguments and Evidence

The Betterment of Humanity

Democratic Despotism

People, Places, and Events

1. *John Adams* (1735-1826) graduated from Harvard in 1755 and was an attorney in Boston when the imperial crisis erupted. He criticized the Stamp Act in a series of newspaper articles and was one of the lawyers who defended the British soldiers tried for murder in the "Boston Massacre" (1770). Adams was, from 1774 to 1778, a delegate from Massachusetts to both the First and Second Continental Congresses. His early thinking on constitutions was published as his *Thoughts on Government* (1776) which had considerable influence among Revolutionary leaders. Adams was the major author of the Massachusetts constitution of 1780, which embodied some of his constitutional ideas.

In his works, Adams argued that the main objective of government was the happiness of the governed. He added that the best form of government was a republic — that is, "an empire of laws, and not of men." The best kind of republic, he continued, would have a legislature of two branches, plus an executive and judiciary so contrived that assembly, governor, and judges would be able to veto the acts of the others. The influence of this on American ideas about government by checks and balances should be obvious. During 1776–1777, Adams urged that the colonies be left to create governments of their own choosing, while a central government be restricted in authority to questions of war, trade, interstate conflicts, and land distribution.

2. *The Articles of Confederation* were, in effect, the first constitution of the United States. Although the Articles were not ratified by all the states until 1781, the central government operated on the basis of the Articles from their formulation in 1777 until the national government was reconstituted in 1789 under the Constitution of 1787.

   Under the Articles, each state had one vote in the Congress, and taxes were apportioned on the basis of the value of surveyed lands in each state. Congress had no power to tax, and so depended on the several states to transmit the apportioned taxes to the central government. Congress was empowered by the Articles to borrow money, issue paper money, make war, conduct diplomatic negotiations, arrange peace, handle Indian affairs, and appoint military and naval officers. By modern standards, the government under the Articles seems surprisingly weak. But Congress directed a war against Great Britain which ended in victory and negotiated a very favorable peace settlement. The land ordinances, as the text points out, resolved the difficult issue of relating dependent territories to the central government.

3. *The Ordinance of 1787,* or Northwest Ordinance, provided for government of the territory north of the Ohio River. The Ordinance of 1785, or Land Ordinance, provided that public lands be surveyed in townships six miles square and divided into thirty-six lots of 640 acres each. Land was to be sold for one dollar an acre in minimum lots of 640 acres. The Northwest Ordinance gave the Northwest Territory a government appointed by Congress. When there were 5,000 adult males in the territory, they could elect members of a lower legislative house and send one nonvoting delegate to Congress. When a population of 60,000 was reached, the inhabitants could draft a constitution and apply for statehood. The new states would be legally equal to the original states. In time, the states of Ohio,

Indiana, Illinois, Michigan, and Wisconsin were formed from the Northwest Territory. Slavery was prohibited in the Territory by the Ordinance.

The Ordinance of 1787 thus solved the problem of relating territories to the rest of the nation, and its principles were applied throughout the American West. It also took a giant step toward dividing the nation into sections over the issue of slavery.

4. *The Order of Cincinnati* was established in 1783 as a hereditary society to perpetuate the honor of the officer corps of the Revolutionary army. Because officers, then as now, represented "gentlemen" socially distinct (at least in theory) from the troops they led, the Cincinnati's formation had social implications. The hereditary features of the order combined with the elitism of the officer corps to suggest that the Revolution had spawned a new artificial aristocracy more suitable to a monarchy than a republic. Public outrage expressed this conviction.

Self-Test

I. Circle the phrase that best completes each statement.

1. When they wrote their new state constitutions during the American Revolution, Americans borrowed and modified the British political system's concept of   (a) constitutional conventions,   (b) separation of powers,   (c) state sovereignty. (227)

2. The state constitutions written in 1776-1777 generally   (a) created weak executives and strong legislatures,   (b) gave equal power to executives, legislatures, and judiciaries,   (c) provided for manhood suffrage. (227-228)

3. Under the Articles of Confederation, the relationship between the national government and the state governments was based upon the concept of   (a) bicameralism,   (b) balanced government,   (c) state sovereignty. (228)

4. The Articles of Confederation provided a central government with   (a) a strong executive,   (b) each state having a single vote in Congress,   (c) the power to levy customs duties to regulate trade. (229)

5. The main reason it took so long for the Articles of Confederation to be ratified by the states was that   (a) the states argued among themselves over who should control western lands,   (b) many states objected that the government under the Articles was too weak,   (c) some states wanted the Articles to abolish slavery. (230)

6. A major triumph of the Articles of Confederation government was the passage of the Ordinance of 1787, which   (a) abolished slavery west of the Mississippi River,   (b) provided for the organization and government of territories,   (c) provided for the surveying and sale of western lands. (231)

7. One result of the Revolution which provided new social and economic opportunities was that   (a) thousands of loyalists left America, leaving their property to be confiscated and sold,   (b) the market for tobacco was considerably expanded,   (c) government regulation of commerce increased. (232)

8. The American Revolution led to the abolition of slavery   (a) in American territories,   (b) by several northern state governments,   (c) by some southern state governments. (243)

9. By the mid-1780s, many American leaders had decided that state legislatures   (a) needed to be strengthened,   (b) should be eliminated,   (c) were the political authority that most threatened liberty. (245)

10. One result of the Revolution was that the state legislatures became   (a) smaller and more elitist in membership,   (b) larger, but represented many narrow political interests,   (c) based on virtual representation. (244)

Answers to the Self-Test

I. 1. b; 2. a; 3. c; 4. b; 5. a; 6. b; 7. a; 8. b; 9. c; 10. b

CHAPTER 10

The Federalist Age

The Historical Problem

This chapter deals with the causes and consequences of the constitutional reform movement of the 1780s. Why did many leaders of the Revolution become dissatisfied with the existing central government under the Articles of Confederation? Why did they question the direction their society was taking? What were the objectives of the constitutional reform movement of the 1780s? Was this reform drive a radical or a reactionary force? What did the movement accomplish? When and why did organized political factions emerge? What did the Federalist administrations of Washington and Adams accomplish? Why did some Americans consider the new national government unrepublican? What did they do about it?

The Historical Problem Answered: The Chapter Thesis

Many leaders came to the conclusion soon after the Revolution that the Confederation government was too weak, and that American society was perverting rather than fulfilling the republican ideal. The central government seemed unable to maintain domestic order or gain international respect. This dissatisfaction produced a nationalist movement that culminated in the writing and ratification of the Constitution of 1787. This new frame of government radically altered the structure of the central government and weakened the power of the states by giving the central government decisive authority and a strong executive.

The Constitution was thus a major victory for the nationalist movement. In defending their creation, the Federalists expanded modern political thinking by analyzing politics in terms of interests rather than the estates of mixed government. The Federalist leaders of the new government, with Alexander Hamilton at their center, tried to reverse the egalitarian thrust of the Revolution by building a centralized, aristocratic empire. A Republican opposition slowly emerged as other American leaders, most notably James Madison and Thomas Jefferson, became concerned that Hamilton's program was creating a corrupt "court" faction. Conflict between Federalists and Republicans reached an inflamed climax in 1798-1799 during the Quasi-War with France, but President John Adams calmed the crisis by refusing to go to war.

The Chain of Arguments and Evidence

The Critical Period

The Federal Constitution

The Hamiltonian Program

The Republican Opposition

People, Places, and Events

1. *James Madison* (1751-1836) was a Virginian who in 1771 graduated
   from the College of New Jersey (Princeton). During the Revolution
   in 1775, Madison served as chairman of a local, extralegal committee
   of public safety for Orange County, Virginia. In the Virginia Convention the next year, Madison helped to draw up the state's Revolutionary constitution. He was a delegate to the Continental Congress
   from 1780 to 1783, an experience that broadened his political hori-
   zons and helped to make him a nationalist. It was Madison who contrived the compromise by which Virginia ceded her western lands to
   the United States, an action that opened the way for the ratification
   of the Articles of Confederation. He was one of those leaders who
   pushed for dramatic alterations in the central government. One of
   the nationalist leaders in the Constitutional Convention of 1787,
   Madison drafted the Virginia Plan which was the basis of the nationalist program. He helped to get the Constitution ratified in Virginia,
   and contributed to the *Federalist Papers* (see next page).

   After the creation of the new national government, James Madison,
   from 1789 to 1797, served as a member of Congress from Virginia.
   With Jefferson, he was a founder of the Republican party and later
   became President of the United States.

2. *Daniel Shays* (1747-1825) was a poor farmer and former Revolutionary army captain who became the leader of a spontaneous uprising of farmers in western Massachusetts in 1786 and 1787. These
   farmers were caught between their debts and the hard times that
   accompanied a postwar economic depression. They asked the Massachusetts legislature to issue paper money to ease the payment of their
   debts or to block the foreclosures that inevitably followed bank-
   ruptcy. The legislature ignored their appeals for relief, and armed
   bands of angry farmers prevented courts from sitting and interrupted
   foreclosures. Under Shays, an armed force of about 1200 attempted
   to capture the arsenal at Springfield, Massachusetts, but was stopped
   by a militia force. After this, the "rebellion" disintegrated, and the
   legislature pardoned all the Shaysites except a few leaders. Even
   Shays was pardoned the next year. This seemingly trivial incident

convinced many leaders that the danger of chaos in America was frighteningly real.

3. *Alexander Hamilton* (1755-1804) was born on the island of Nevis in the British West Indies. After an unhappy childhood, Hamilton was aided in his migration to New York where, in 1773, he entered King's College (later Columbia University).

Swept up in the Revolutionary movement, Hamilton took the patriot side and organized an artillery company when war broke out. He was a young man of keen intellect and considerable ability. It was natural for Washington to make Hamilton his aide-de-camp, a post he held from 1777 to 1781. A man on the rise, Hamilton married into the Schuyler family, one of the most wealthy and politically powerful in the state of New York. He served in Congress in 1782–1783 and became one of the most ardent nationalists in support of a much stronger central government. The Constitution of 1787 did not create a government sufficiently powerful and centralized to suit him, but Hamilton supported the Constitution as the strongest national government obtainable under the circumstances. He contributed importantly to the *Federalist Papers* (see below) and worked to ensure New York's ratification of the Constitution.

When Hamilton became the first secretary of the treasury, he and his policies became central to the development of political divisions and political conflict in the early national period. Even after his resignation from the cabinet in 1795, Hamilton remained a force in national politics and contributed to the splintering of the Federalist party. An enigmatic and controversial figure in his own day and in the arguments of historians, Hamilton was the central nationalist leader from the adoption of the Constitution to 1800. He died tragically in July 1804 after being wounded in a duel with Vice-President Aaron Burr.

4. *The Federalist Papers* are a series of essays in support of ratification of the Constitution. Eighty-five of them appeared in New York newspapers in 1787 and 1788. James Madison wrote about twenty-eight; John Jay wrote five; and Alexander Hamilton composed the remainder. These discussions of the Constitution were designed to aid the Federalist side in the New York convention. Although it is doubtful that they had any decisive impact, they remain perhaps the most brilliant and certainly the most extensive discussion of the new government and its political principles by leading proponents of the Constitution. The tenth paper (by Madison) is still considered by many scholars to be the most profound discussion, written by an American, of the dynamics of politics in a republican government.

5. *John Jay* (1745-1829) graduated from King's College (later Columbia University) in 1764 and practiced law in New York. A moderate during the Revolutionary crisis, Jay served as a delegate from New York to the First and Second Continental Congresses. He chaired the committee that drafted the New York state constitution of 1777. A member of the United States delegation that negotiated peace with Britain at the end of the War for American Independence, Jay served as the secretary of foreign affairs in the Confederation government from 1784 to 1790. A strong nationalist, Jay supported the Constitution of 1787 and contributed to the *Federalist Papers*. He was appointed the first chief justice of the new Supreme Court.

   Jay's most controversial activity in a long and busy public career came in 1794 when he was dispatched to Britain by the Washington administration to negotiate the issues that were disturbing the relations between the two countries. Jay's conduct of these negotiations is variously evaluated by historians. Some think that he did as well as could be expected, considering the fact that he lacked any diplomatic leverage to exert on Britain. Others think that Jay was so eager to reach any kind of settlement with Britain that he did not use what few advantages he did have. In any case, the resulting Jay's Treaty, when its terms were made public in 1795, caused a storm of bitter political dispute in the United States.

   From the Federalist point of view, the treaty paid a reasonable price for peace with Britain; from the Republican point of view, the treaty sold out American self-respect for nothing. By the treaty, Britain agreed to evacuate the military posts in American territory that she still occupied in violation of the Treaty of Paris (1783). Problems of pre-Revolutionary debts, boundaries, and maritime seizures were to be referred to joint commissions. The treaty did prevent an impending war and was ratified by the Senate by an exact two-thirds majority. Some historians believe that the storm over Jay's Treaty was the decisive event in the creation of the Republican party. Jay survived the excitement, resigned from the Supreme Court, and served two terms as governor of New York before retiring in 1800.

6. *The Alien and Sedition Acts* consisted of four measures passed in June and July, 1798. The Naturalization Act extended the period of residency required for citizenship from five to fourteen years. The Alien Act empowered the president to deport dangerous aliens. The Alien Enemies Act gave the president power to arrest or deport subjects of a hostile nation in time of war. The Sedition Act made it a crime, among other things, to publish "false, scandalous and malicious" writings against the United States government, Congress,

or the president. Republicans protested that the last act made it illegal to criticize the government. The Adams administration left no doubt about what the purpose was; ten persons were convicted under provisions of the Sedition Act, and all ten were Republican editors and printers. Thomas Jefferson, when president, pardoned all those convicted under the Sedition Act.

Self-Test

I. Match each identifying statement with the appropriate name.

a. John Fries (271)   e. John Jay (267)
b. Thomas Jefferson (253)   f. James Madison (254, 265)
c. Robert Morris (249)   g. John Adams (271)
d. Daniel Shays (252)   h. Alexander Hamilton (261)

1. __f__ A leading nationalist in the 1780s who played a central role in the Constitutional Convention, but became a leading opponent of the Federalist administration from his seat in the House of Representatives in the 1790s.

2. __a__ Emerged as the leader of debt-ridden, angry, and insurgent farmers in western Massachusetts in the winter of 1786–1787.

3. __h__ President Washington's influential secretary of treasury who made himself a key figure in the new government by designing a program to tie wealth to the new national government and thus assure its stability.

4. __b__ Although one of the most important Revolutionary leaders, he was not present at the Constitutional Convention because he was on a diplomatic mission in France.

5. __e__ An experienced American diplimat, he was, nonetheless, burned in effigy when the terms of a treaty he negotiated with the British in 1793 were made public.

II. Circle the phrase that best completes each statement.

1. The problems of the "Critical Period" in the 1780s appeared most critical to (a) states' rightists, (b) nationalists, (c) localists. (249)

2. Differences between the interests of Northeasterners and Southwesterners helped defeat the ratification of (a) the Jay-Gardoqui Treaty, (b) Jay's Treaty, (c) Pinckney's Treaty. (251)

3. The delegates to the Constitutional Convention were (a) well educated, (b) politically inexperienced, (c) representative of the whole population. (253)

4. The basic features of the Constitution of 1787 were originally contained in (a) the Virginia Plan, (b) the New Jersey Plan, (c) the Articles of Confederation. (253-255)

5. Perhaps the most controversial issue in the Constitutional Convention was the question of (a) whether there should be a one-house or a two-house legislature, (b) giving the central government the power to levy taxes, (c) proportional representation in the legislature. (255)

6. Antifederalists attacked the new Constitution as a threat to (a) popular sovereignty, (b) separation of powers, (c) state sovereignty. (256)

7. Alexander Hamilton's legislative program included all of the following proposals *except* (a) funding of the national debt, (b) subsidies for grain farmers, (c) protective tariffs to encourage manufacturing. (260-263)

8. Generally, the Republicans feared (a) strict constructionists, (b) French influence in America, (c) energetic government. (265-266)

9. The Republicans' response to the Alien and Sedition Acts was the (a) Proclamation of Neutrality, (b) Kentucky and Virginia Resolutions, (c) XYZ Affair. (271)

Answers to the Self-Test

I. 1. f; 2. d; 3. h; 4. b; 5. e
II. 1. b; 2. a; 3. a; 4. a; 5. c; 6. c; 7. b; 8. c; 9. b

CHAPTER 11

The Revolution Recovered

The Historical Problem

The problem is to understand and explain Republicanism's impact on
and accomplishments in domestic society and foreign policy. In what sense
was the election of 1800 a revolution? What was the ideology of the
Republicans? How did Republican ideology influence Republican policies
once in power? What were the domestic and foreign policy consequences
of Republican rule?

The Historical Problem Answered: The Chapter Thesis

The Republicans thought their victory in 1800 represented a genuine
revolution. Republican control of the government meant that Federalist
programs could be blocked, and that the most important libertarian goal
could be achieved by reducing the power of government. The Republicans
set out to create a government that would operate without depending
on privileges and patronage. Their success increased political confusion
and weakened the power of the national executive. Jefferson's acquisition of the Louisiana Territory also fulfilled his dream of a western "empire
of liberty."

At the same time, it was widely believed that Protestantism, even though
divided into numerous denominations, was the cement that held American
society together. The Revolution heightened the millenial impulse within
American Protestantism, and the Second Great Awakening spread evangelicalism even more widely. The Revolutionary period's classical ideal of
virtue was thus now evangelized.

In foreign policy, the Republicans also attempted to implement the
libertarian ideals of the Revolutionary generation. Caught between France

and Great Britain, the Republicans tried to defend their principles of foreign relations, but they were finally driven into war with Britain. The War of 1812 seemed to complete the American Revolution: the Federalists were shattered, the united republic was saved, and an "Era of Good Feelings" seemed to have begun.

The Chain of Arguments and Evidence

People, Places, and Events

1. *Meriwether Lewis* (1774-1809) and *William Clark* (1770-1838) are certainly the two most famous American explorers, and deservedly so. Both were army officers and Virginians. Lewis was President Jefferson's private secretary and was chosen by Jefferson to lead an overland exploration to the Pacific. Lewis selected Clark to join him, and the two shared the burdens of leadership.

   In the spring of 1804, they led a party of twenty-five men up the Missouri River and then wintered among the Mandan Indians in what is now central North Dakota. When spring came in 1805, they crossed the Rocky Mountains and descended the Columbia River to the Pacific. There they spent the winter of 1805-1806. The party then recrossed the mountains, partly by different routes, and arrived in St. Louis in September 1806. Along the way, the party collected geographical information, drew maps, and recorded scientific data about plants, animals, and the geology of the regions they had traversed. It was a promising start for government promotion of scientific inquiry; yet most of the materials gathered by Lewis and Clark went unused until the end of the nineteenth century.

   After their great adventure, Lewis was appointed governor of the Louisiana Territory, and Clark was made superintendent of Indian Affairs in St. Louis, a post he held until his death in 1838. William Clark also served as the appointed governor of Missouri Territory from 1813 until statehood in 1821. Meriweather Lewis died in 1809 at the age of thirty-five under circumstances suggesting either suicide or murder.

2. *Aaron Burr* (1756-1836) is one of the more enigmatic of the leaders of the early republic. He was born in New Jersey and was graduated from the College of New Jersey (later Princeton University) in 1772. During the War for American Independence, Burr served primarily as a staff officer and rose to the rank of lieutenant colonel. After the war, he practiced law in New York and was attorney general of the state until he was elected to the United States Senate where he served from 1791 to 1797. Burr and Hamilton were bitter political rivals in New York. Burr tied with Jefferson in the electoral college vote in 1800. Repetition of this problem was resolved by the Twelfth Amendment, which changed the method of voting for president and vice-president. Burr was dropped from the Republican ticket in 1804 after serving as Jefferson's first vice-president. In the same year, Burr challenged Alexander Hamilton to a duel after the latter had published some political charges against him. In the duel Burr mortally wounded Hamilton.

Burr later concocted a plan that remains one of the most intriguing mysteries in American history. He began gathering an armed party in the West in order to descend the Mississippi. It is not clear whether the purpose of the expedition was to provoke the secession of the western states from the Union or to detach a portion of northern Mexico. It is quite possible that Burr did not know what his object was. In any case, he was arrested, charged with treason, and acquitted by Chief Justice John Marshall, much to the chagrin of President Jefferson. After a period of residence in Europe, this odd child of the Revolution returned to practice law in New York City.

3. *John Marshall* (1755-1835) was the most influential jurist ever to lead the Supreme Court. Born in Virginia, Marshall served in the army under Washington until 1781. He was admitted to the Virginia bar and served in the Virginia legislature. He supported ratification of the Constitution of 1787 in Virginia and became a Federalist leader there. Appointed minister to France in 1797, Marshall became involved in the XYZ Affair. John Adams appointed Marshall to the Supreme Court as chief justice just before he left office. Marshall served thirty-four years on the High Court and, during most of the time, he was its leader.

   The Marshall Court first declared a congressional act unconstitutional in *Marbury* v. *Madison* (1803), declared state laws invalid in *Fletcher* v. *Peck* (1810), protected the right of contract in *Dartmouth College* v. *Woodward* (1819), accepted the broad constructionism of implied powers in *McCulloch* v. *Maryland* (1819), and extended federal control over interstate commerce in *Gibbons* v. *Ogden* (1824). Marshall helped to make the Court a central nationalist institution. He died in office.

4. *Deists* were men and women who believed that traditional Christian orthodoxy had hardened into an obscurantist creed that concealed the clear and simple truths of a rational religion. Deists were not atheists, for they believed in an impersonal divinity, or first cause, the creator of the universe. They thought that the proper way to worship this prime mover was to do good for mankind on earth. They believed that it was possible to live a virtuous life without the aid of institutional religion and without supernatural sanctions. Most deists also believed that there would be a life hereafter in which virtue would be rewarded and wickedness punished. Deists attempted to establish ethical principles apart from the supernatural. They did not think it necessary to have organized churches, sacraments, ceremonies, or a ministry. Such leading men as Benjamin Franklin and

Thomas Jefferson were deists, but these ideas appealed to a relatively small portion of the American population.

5. *The Second Great Awakening* at the turn of the century was fed by the embers of the original Great Awakening (1739-1745), which had never completely died out in America. One expression of the Second Great Awakening was a frontier revival, led by James McGready, that climaxed at a camp meeting held at Cane Ridge, Kentucky, in August 1801. The camp meeting was devised as a way to evangelize people who were dispersed in rural settlements and scattered frontier farms. Instead of bringing the revival to the people, the people were brought to the revival which was held at a "camp" constructed for the purpose. There the revival could go on day and night without interruption for anywhere from three to as long as seven days. This naturally heightened the emotional intensity of the revival experience, which often led to unrestrained displays of barking and jerking that discredited the revivals among some eastern churchmen. The Second Great Awakening also affected Yale College, and revivalists from the school provided leadership for the rekindling of evangelical enthusiasm in New York and New England.

6. *"Denominationalism"* is the term used to describe the peculiar organization of American churches and to define the differences between the major religious groups in America and traditional churches in Europe. American denominations are based on voluntarism rather than state establishment; they include only those who wish to be members. The Protestant church groups do not claim that they have an exclusive hold on religious truths; on the contrary, they argue that many different groups are but separate denominations of a larger Christian whole. Denominationalism meant that American churches could multiply and splinter, yet agree on basic religious teachings.

Self-Test

I. March each identifying statement with the appropriate name.

a. Aaron Burr (286)   e. Tippecanoe (287)
b. Tecumseh (287)   f. John Pickering (288)
c. Henry Clay (299)   g. Samuel Chase (288)
d. Thomas Jefferson (298)

1. _____ His conviction that the republic should use commerce rather than military force to assert its rights in international affairs was most dramatically expressed in the Embargo of 1807.

2. _____ The conflict with his Indian confederacy in late 1811 convinced many that British and Spanish bases in Canada and
Florida had to be eliminated.

3. _____ A victim of the Republican effort to bring the federal judiciary
under greater congressional control, he was impeached and
removed from office for "high crimes and misdemeanors."

4. _____ A newly elected Republican congressman who, in 1810,
came to Congress as a "War Hawk" eager for the United
States to take military action against the British.

II. Match each identifying statement with one of the items below.

    a. deism (291)   e. impressment (296)
    b. strict construction (285)   f. Judiciary Act of 1789 (289)
    c. Judiciary Act of 1801 (288)   g. judicial review (288)
    d. millennialism (294)   h. peaceful coercion (296, 300)

1. _____ The act of Congress that was ruled unconstitutional by Chief
Justice John Marshall and the Supreme Court in 1803.

2. _____ An historic British naval practice that Americans found
exasperating which was eventually cited by President Madison
as a cause for war in 1812.

3. _____ It contributed to the nation's growing sense of mission by
alleging that America was leading mankind into an age of
glory.

4. _____ The principle of government dearly held by most Republicans,
it was, nevertheless, consciously violated by the Louisiana
Purchase in 1803.

III. Circle the phrase that best completes each statement.

1. Once they gained office, the Republicans   (a) adopted the programs
and policies of the Federalists,   (b) undertook new departures
in the area of social welfare programs,   (c) reduced the pomp and
power of the central government. (280)

2. The most popular event of Jefferson's presidency was the   (a) Burr
conspiracy,   (b) Louisiana Purchase,   (c) Embargo Act. (285)

3. An act of Congress was first declared unconstitutional in
(a) *McCulloch* v. *Maryland,*   (b) *Marbury* v. *Madison,*
(c) *Fletcher* v. *Peck.* (289)

4. The Second Great Awakening   (a) was most successful in the West,   (b) reestablished the orthodoxy of the Congregational Church in New England,   (c) demarcated a clear distinction between Christian religion and Republican ideology in America. (293)

5. American anxiety and frustration over British violations of American maritime rights reached a climax in   (a) the rule of 1756, (b) the *Chesapeake-Leopard* affair,   (c) Macon's Bill No. 2. (298)

6. Federalist opposition to the War of 1812 was clearly expressed in the   (a) Treaty of Ghent,   (b) *Essex* decision,   (c) Hartford Convention. (302)

Answers to the Self-Test

  I. 1. d; 2. b; 3. f; 4. c
 II. 1. f; 2. e; 3. d; 4. b
III. 1. c; 2. b; 3. b; 4. a; 5. b; 6. c

PART THREE

David Brion Davis *Expanding the Republic*

1820–1860

Thesis

The end of the Enlightenment stopped further efforts to model American society on European examples. America was now to be a nation without traditional distinctions of rank and without traditional restraints. Americans had come to believe that individual pursuit of self-interest would best promote the public good. The energies thus released produced economic growth, territorial expansion, and a foreign policy largely concerned with the acquisition of land and the prevention of European interference with the extension of American influence. State and national governments encouraged territorial expansion and economic growth. Political ideology focused on removing institutions that seemed to limit individual opportunity.

Many Americans worried that this expansive individualism would lead to social chaos and crass materialism, and they moved to prevent this by promoting the moral reformation of individuals. The drive for moral improvement helped to modernize American society, because it encouraged behavior that gave a larger meaning to a market-oriented society. The question of Negro slavery illustrated the value conflict between flourishing self-interest and the ideal of righteousness that inspired Americans. The issue of the westward expansion of slavery became the critical test for defining the limits of a society without bounds. The unavoidable question for Americans became whether any limits could be placed on one person's dominion of another.

Chronology

1823	Monroe Doctrine issued
1825	National religious revivals begin
1828	Election of Andrew Jackson
1846–1848	Mexican-American War
1850	Compromise of 1850
1851	Herman Melville's *Moby Dick* published
1854	Kansas-Nebraska Act; Whig party collapses
1859	John Brown's raid on Harper's Ferry, Virginia
1860	Election of Lincoln; South Carolina secedes

CHAPTER 12

Population: Expansion and Exploitation

The Historical Problem

The problem is to understand the special features and distinctive quality of American life from 1820 to 1860. How did population growth and economic changes affect American society during this period? What conditions encouraged these demographic and economic changes and shaped their social consequences? What were the causes of population growth? What were the causes of economic changes? What produced the westward movement? In what ways did these changes prove liberating? In what ways did they prove disruptive?

The Historical Problem Answered: The Chapter Thesis

The distinctive feature of American development in the years from 1820 to 1860 is the emergence of a modern market economy in conjunction with the settlement of land in the West. Population grew rapidly in the period, and there were few obstacles to economic and territorial expansion. Immigration was unlimited, and government policy encouraged the rapid settlement of virgin land. There were few restraints on the operation of the market economy. Although there were no sudden economic departures, investments of land, labor, and capital produced rapid economic growth.

The first stages of industrialization had begun. Self-sufficient farming declined, and household manufacturing nearly disappeared. Agriculture increasingly devoted itself to cash crops for urban and industrial markets. Industrial achievements sprang from labor-saving technology and exploitation of cheap resources. These changes liberated men and women from older ties and increased the possibilities of individual choice. The standard of living rose and, at the same time, economic inequalities increased. But the nation's economic and territorial expansion also involved the racial exploitation of black slaves and native American Indians.

The Chain of Arguments and Evidence

People, Places, and Events

1. *The Cherokee Indians* originally inhabited what is now western North Carolina and South Carolina, northern Georgia, and eastern Tennessee. They lived in villages scattered on both sides of the southern Appalachians. Similar in many ways to other Woodlands Indians of the Southeast, the Cherokees supported a class of priests, *hopoye,* who exorcised the evil spirits that caused sickness and who supervised the religious life of the people. A major ceremony was the green corn festival that was widely celebrated among southeastern tribes. With other tribes of the Southeast, the Cherokee came to be referred to by whites as the "Five Civilized Tribes." In 1827, the Cherokees

were the last eastern tribe of any strength. Treaties with the United States since 1791 had recognized the Cherokees as a "nation." Consequently, Cherokees met at New Echota, Georgia, to draft a constitution that would create an Indian state. Georgia urged instead that the federal government remove the Cherokees from their state.

The conflict led to a Supreme Court case, *Cherokee Nation* v. *Georgia* (1831), where the Indians sought an injunction to prevent Georgia from enforcing state laws in Indian territory. The Court decided that the Cherokees held their lands only by right of occupancy, and that they did not have the status of a nation. In *Worcester* v. *Georgia,* decided the next year, Chief Justice Marshall declared that the state had no right to molest the tribe; but President Jackson refused to use presidential authority to protect the Indians from white violations. In 1835, a minority of the Cherokees signed a treaty ceding all of the tribal lands to the United States in exchange for land in the Indian Territory west of the Mississippi, transportation costs, and $5 million. The march to the West caused enormous suffering and the deaths of about one-quarter of the tribe.

2. *Seminole Indian Wars* (1818-1819; 1835-1842) The Seminole Indians lived in Florida, and conflict with Americans broke out along the southern border of Georgia. Escaped slaves found sanctuary of sorts among the Seminoles, and tribesmen occasionally raided settlements along the border. In 1818, Andrew Jackson led a military force into Spanish Florida to punish the Indians. One result was an international incident when Jackson hanged two British subjects in the area that was under Spanish jurisdiction. Another result was that sufficient pressure was applied by this military action to convince Spain that she might as well negotiate the sale of Florida to the United States before the Americans simply seized it.

The later Seminole War took place when Indians resisted the government's efforts to implement the removal policy. Most of the Seminoles did not want to exchange their lands in Florida, now under United States jurisdiction, for lands west of the Mississippi. The long war ended in a treaty in 1842, which allowed some Seminoles to remain in Florida. The most famous Indian leader, Osceola, was captured while protected by a flag of truce; he died in prison. Other Indians were killed during the conflict or moved to the Indian Territory. Spreading white settlements forced the remaining Seminoles to retreat into the Everglades region of south Florida, where their descendants still live.

3. *Erie Canal* Construction on this most famous and economically important of all American canals began in 1817 and was completed

in 1825. The canal made it possible for goods to be shipped from the Great Lakes to the port of New York. The canal cut across New York state from Buffalo to Albany, a distance of 364 difficult miles. Construction cost $7 million but tolls paid the interest charges on the loans before the canal was completed. Travel time from Buffalo to New York City was reduced from twenty days to six days; freight rates were reduced from one hundred dollars to five dollars a ton. The completion of the canal enabled the port of New York to serve the entire Middle West and it stimulated the economic development of western New York state. The Erie Canal encouraged the construction of other canals, but few were as successful.

4. *John Jacob Astor* (1763-1848) was the founder of one of the great American fortunes that makes his name still synonymous with enormous wealth. Astor was born in Germany and migrated to London and then to the United States as a youth. In New York City in 1784, he went to work in a fur store and moved into the fur business on his own. He prospered by trading furs, began buying New York City real estate, and traded with China. In 1808, Astor organized the American Fur Company capitalized at $1 million to monopolize the fur trade in the American West recently acquired by the Louisiana Purchase. In 1813, Astor was in a position to loan the United States government $2 million. After the War of 1812, Astor monopolized the fur trade of the upper Missouri valley. He retired from fur trading in 1834 and devoted his energies to financial arrangements and New York real estate. At his death, his fortune amounted to at least $20 million; it remains largely in the hands of the Astor family.

5. *The Nat Turner Insurrection* took place in Southampton County, Virginia in August 1831. Nat Turner was a slave whose religious "experience" helped make him a spiritual leader among the slaves of the area. By all accounts, Turner was a model slave and was unusually religious. The origins of the insurrection apparently lay in the religious life of Nat Turner, which may have convinced him that he was chosen by God to free his people from bondage. The slave uprising shattered the confident calm of Virginia with unimaginable violence. The revolting slaves killed fifty-seven white men, women, and children. Then the whites retaliated, killing perhaps as many as one hundred blacks in a spectacular manhunt. Twenty more blacks, including Nat Turner, were executed after being tried. The psychological impact of the insurrection resulted in part from the fact that it made a bloody reality out of the slave society's worst nightmare, a slave uprising.

Self-Test

I. Match each identifying statement with the appropriate name.

a. Horace Greeley (335)　　　　e. Alexis de Tocqueville (315, 334)
b. Nat Turner (329)　　　　　　f. Denmark Vesey (329)
c. John Marshall (323)　　　　　g. William Henry Harrison (322)
d. George Catlin (324)

1. _____ One of several European travelers in early nineteenth-century America who was struck by the amazing mobility of America's restless population.

2. _____ Chief Justice of the Supreme Court who ruled in *Worcester* v. *Georgia* that the Cherokees need not be subject to state laws.

3. _____ His victory over the Shawnees in the Old Northwest together with Andrew Jackson's defeat of the Creeks opened the way to white exploitation of tribal divisions and Congress's removal policy.

4. _____ Leader of one of the Old South's bloodiest slave revolts in Southampton County, Virginia in 1831.

II. Circle the phrase that best completes each statement.

1. Immigration in the early nineteenth century was largely a function of America's   (a) economic prosperity,   (b) political freedom,   (c) religious liberty. (312-313)

2. American immigration between 1840 and 1860 flowed mainly from   (a) southern and eastern Europe,   (b) central Europe,   (c) northern and western Europe. (313)

3. Among the other consequences of the rapid settlement of virgin lands in the period 1820-1860 was   (a) the weakening of cities as population flowed to the West,   (b) the adoption of federal land-use laws to control growth,   (c) the abuse and thoughtless exploitation of soil, forests, and other resources. (316-317)

4. The chief business of the central government in the early nineteenth century was   (a) the regulation of the economy,   (b) the management and sale of public lands,   (c) railroad construction. (317)

5. State "occupancy laws" were often passed to protect the land claims of   (a) Indians,   (b) land speculators,   (c) squatters. (317)

6. In the early nineteenth century, American Indian policy was based, among other things, on the proposition that   (a) Indian occupancy must give way to white settlement,   (b) the Indians were citizens of the states where they resided,   (c) the federal government had no business dealing with the Indians. (323)

7. Antebellum slavery was characterized by   (a) unrelieved violence and brutality,   (b) strong community ties among the slaves, (c) the disintegration of black family life. (331)

8. In the early nineteenth century, the age of the "common man" was celebrated   (a) because wealth was so evenly distributed, (b) because it was relatively easy for the poor to attain wealth, (c) despite the fact that there were growing inequities in the distribution of wealth. (332)

9. Efforts to organize the labor force in early nineteenth-century America were most effective among   (a) unskilled immigrants,   (b) skilled craftsmen,   (c) white collar workers. (335)

Answers to the Self-Test

I. 1. e; 2. c; 3. g; 4. b
II. 1. a; 2. c; 3. c; 4. b; 5. c; 6. a; 7. b; 8. c; 9. b

CHAPTER 13

Politics: Cohesion and Division

The Historical Problem

The problem is to define and explain the nature of American politics in a republic of limitless opportunity. What political issues arose? What political parties appeared? What purposes did the parties serve? What common features did the parties share? What was the new American political style? What were the limitations of the party system?

The Historical Problem Answered: The Chapter Thesis

It became increasingly clear during the mid-1820s that the republican ideal of a unified harmonious family was not relevant to new social realities. Economic growth and territorial expansion multiplied the number of groups competing for opportunity and for favorable government policies. The Missouri Compromise demonstrated slavery's potential for destroying the republican experiment by producing bitter division. And the later Nullification Crisis revealed the possibilities for sectional conflict over economic policies like the tariff, especially when combined with the slavery issue. The Van Buren Republicans of New York state offered a new kind of political party capable of serving as an agent of the people and of unifying the republic. Thus Americans organized their divisions by constructing a national two-party system. The political party system succeeded in preserving national unity from the early 1830s to the early 1850s. Political leaders appealed to the coalition of interest groups that made up the parties for support against some privileged special interest charged with closing off opportunity.

Andrew Jackson became the first popular political leader to gain a national following. In office, the Democrats waged war against the Bank of the United States, a "monster institution" that allegedly limited opportunity. Jacksonian efforts to demolish the barriers to individual enterprise unintentionally opened the door for the expansion of *laissez-faire* capitalism. Although the Whig party mastered the techniques of the new democratic politics, the party was not able to find a national leader to rival Andrew Jackson. In addition, the reform Whigs disapproved of the compromises required for political success. The party system worked, but only so long as it ignored the explosive question of slavery.

The Chain of Arguments and Evidence

	TEXT PAGES
1. What was the traditional assumption about political parties?	339

"A Fire Bell in the Night": The Missouri Compromise

1. Why was slavery *not* a national political issue before 1819?	341
2. What was the Missouri crisis?	342
3. What changed conditions produced the Missouri crisis?	342
4. What were the elements of the Missouri Compromise?	343
5. What were the consequences of the Missouri crisis and Compromise?	343-344

The End of Republican Unity

1. How did the Missouri Compromise influence attitudes toward political parties?	344
2. What did Martin Van Buren and the "Bucktails" contribute to the idea of political parties?	344
3. Why did the Republicans fall into disunity?	344
4. Who were the candidates, and what were the issues in the election of 1824?	344-345
a. Who was Andrew Jackson?	345-346
5. How did the election affect the Republican party?	346

Jackson's Rise to Power

1. How are Jackson's political strength and the Democratic party's appeal to be explained?	346-347
2. What is the significance of Jackson's 1828 victory?	347
3. What was the "spoils" system?	347
4. What were the functions and significance of the party convention?	348

6. What made the Whig party particularly vulnerable to
   cultural and sectional issues?
7. What were the limitations of the two-party political
   system?

People, Places, and Events

1. *John Quincy Adams* (1767-1848), son of John Adams, carried on
   his family's tradition of leadership in foreign affairs and politics.
   After being educated in Europe and America (Adams was graduated
   from Harvard in 1787), he studied law and began a diplomatic career.
   He served as United States minister to the Netherlands (1794-1796)
   and then as minister to Prussia (1797-1801), while his father was
   president. Adams left the Federalist party of his father and served as
   minister to Russia (1809-1814) under the Republicans. He participated in the negotiations that resulted in the Treaty of Ghent which
   ended the War of 1812.

   Under President Monroe, John Quincy Adams distinguished himself
   as one of the most able and effective American secretaries of state. The
   Adams-Onís Treaty secured Florida from Spain and extinguished Spain's
   claims to the Pacific Northwest. Adams shaped the Monroe Doctrine
   in 1823, and conceived of America's future in the broadest terms.

   John Quincy Adams failed as president partly because his conception of government as an agent of national cultural integration was
   in advance of his times. After those unhappy years, Adams served
   from 1831 to 1848 as a member of the House of Representatives
   from the Plymouth district of Massachusetts. From his House seat
   he opposed the expansion of slavery into the territories. He died in
   the capitol building in 1848.

2. *Martin Van Buren* (1782-1862), born in Kinderhook, New York,
   was destined for a life in politics. He was a lawyer who became in-
   volved in local politics, serving as state senator and attorney general.
   By 1820, he had become the leader of the Democratic party in New
   York, organized as the "Albany Regency." He served in the United
   States Senate from 1820 to 1828 and he helped Jackson win in New
   York in 1828. Jackson appointed Van Buren secretary of state and
   then selected the New Yorker to be his vice-presidential running mate
   in 1832. His reddish hair occasioned one of his many nicknames,
   "The Red Fox of Kinderhook," which also suggested his well-earned
   reputation for political sagacity.

   Van Buren inherited the leadership of the Jacksonian movement
   in 1836, but his presidential years unfortunately coincided with an

economic slump, and he was unable to beat the Whig, William Henry Harrison, in 1840. He opposed the extension of slavery into the territories in his post-presidential years, and he even ran in 1848 as the Free Soil party's candidate for president. He retired soon after, a major contributor to the practice of modern democratic politics.

3. *Nicholas Biddle* (1786-1844) was one of the central figures in the famous "Bank War" of 1832-1833; the other was Andrew Jackson. He was a native Philadelphian whose connection to the Second Bank of the United States has obscured his importance as a literary figure. Biddle was graduated from the College of New Jersey (later Princeton University) in 1801 at the age of fifteen.

After serving as secretary to American diplomats in Paris and London, he returned to Philadelphia in 1807, where he edited a magazine called *Port Folio* and helped edit the journals of the Lewis and Clark expedition (published in 1814). President Monroe, whom Biddle had earlier served as secretary when Monroe was United States minister to Great Britain, appointed his former secretary to be one of the government directors of the Second Bank of the United States in 1816. Biddle was chosen bank president in 1822, and he held that post until he retired in 1839.

His conservative fiscal policies antagonized those who favored an easy money policy. Biddle's efforts to have the Second Bank act as a central bank, stabilizing and moderating economic fluctuations, stimulated the opposition of small businessmen and local bankers. His fatal mistake was in applying for a renewal of the bank's charter in 1832 when the original charter did not expire for another four years. He gained the support of such Whig leaders as Henry Clay and Daniel Webster, thereby guaranteeing that the recharter bill would become a political issue in the presidential contest.

Jackson's political popularity and Biddle's failure to understand the political realities of the day assured the defeat of the bank bill. In 1836, the bank was chartered by Pennsylvania when its original national charter expired, but the bank collapsed in 1841. Sadly, Biddle lost his own money and was tried on criminal charges. He died in 1844, the most spectacular casualty of the Bank War and the politics of opportunity.

4. *Independent Treasury* President Van Buren's plan for an Independent Treasury was designed to separate government finances from the private banking system. The Independent Treasury Act established government depositories independent of state banks. This act was passed in 1840 despite fervent Whig opposition. After their victory in the 1840 election, the Whigs repealed the Independent Treasury

Act in 1841 as part of their preparations for the creation of a national bank to replace the Second Bank of the Untied States. When the Democrats regained power in 1844, they passed the Independent Treasury Act of 1846 which was substantially the same as the 1840 measure. The act provided that the Treasury would keep government funds in treasury and sub-treasury offices and accept only specie (hard money) or treasury notes. This divorced the Treasury from the banking system and served as the basis of the government fiscal system until the Civil War, when the National Banking System was established in 1863 by the Lincoln administration.

5. *Log Cabins and Hard Cider*   The presidential election campaign of 1840 is a particularly interesting and important one because of the unusual political excitement and the exuberance with which all parties used the popular devices that had been developed for attracting voter interest. Political rallies, songs, banners, processions, and hoopla were well and widely used. The log cabin, hard cider, and coonskin cap, all supposedly symbols of a rural, rustic, simple, democratic background, were effectively employed by the Whigs to steal the Democratic party's democratic image. Good party organization by the Whigs, and the economic slump following the financial panic of 1837, also helped William Henry Harrison defeat Martin Van Buren. Harrison died shortly after his inauguration, but the political techniques lived on.

Self-Test

I. Match each identifying statement with the appropriate name.

a. Nicholas Biddle (352, 354)
b. Daniel Webster (357)
c. John C. Calhoun (357-358)
d. Martin Van Buren (344)
e. William H. Crawford (344)
f. William Henry Harrison (359-360)
g. John Quincy Adams (346)
h. Thurlow Weed (359)
i. Henry Clay (343, 351)

1. _____ The Whig party's successful presidential candidate in 1840 who was elected by their successful application of campaign tactics originally worked out by the Democrats.

2. _____ Leader of the "bucktail" faction of New York politics who implemented a new conception of political parties as agents of the peoples' interests.

3. _____ His election to the presidency was accompanied by a charge of a "corrupt bargain" that helped make his national leadership ineffective.

4. _____ President of the Second Bank of the United States who, after the veto of its recharter bill, tried to create a small financial panic to demonstrate the bank's importance.

5. _____ Powerful senator from Massachusetts who supported the recharter bill and was a major leader of the Whig opposition to President Jackson.

6. _____ Skillful senator from Kentucky who managed a compromise solution to both the Missouri Crisis in 1819 and the Nullification Crisis in 1832.

II. Match each identifying statement with one of the items below.

a. specie circular (354)   f. American system (344, 357)
b. spoils system (347)   g. Kitchen Cabinet (349)
c. nullification (350)   h. internal improvements (344)
d. natural law (342)   i. gag rule (351)
e. caucus system (344, 348)

1. _____ A concept appealed to by Northerners who opposed the admission of Missouri as a slave state in 1819.

2. _____ The doctrine appealed to by South Carolinians who opposed the Tariff of 1832.

3. _____ A plan designed to reduce American dependence on foreign trade by advocating government aid to promote American economic development.

4. _____ A way of rotating public offices among loyal party members, it was also hailed as a way to more completely democratize the national government.

5. _____ Used by Congress as a way to prevent the introduction of antislavery petitions into congressional debate in the 1830s and early 1840s.

III. Circle the phrase that best completes each statement.

1. The Missouri Compromise seemed to settle the future of slavery in (a) the Northwest Territory, (b) the Old Southwest, (c) the Louisiana Territory. (343)

2. Jackson's national political appeal in the campaign of 1828 depended on all of the following factors *except* (a) his reputation as a successful, but plain man of the people, (b) his clear and articulate

analysis of the public issues of the day,   (c) his reputation as a soldier. (346-347)

3. The Jacksonian financial policy was   (a) to rely on hard money, (b) to rely on a national banking system,   (c) to replace gold specie with paper currency. (352)

4. To Jackson, the Second Bank of the United States   (a) amounted to a government subsidy to the wealthy and powerful,   (b) would have been acceptable if it had been controlled by the government, (c) was constitutional but inefficient. (353)

5. A supporter of laissez-faire, President Jackson   (a) allowed Congress to gain power at the executive's expense,   (b) used executive power forcefully to counter artificial concentrations of power, (c) was relatively inactive and passive as a national leader. (356)

6. Whigs generally supported the view that America's economic problems could be more effectively dealt with by   (a) aggressive territorial expansion,   (b) constant technological improvements,   (c) unregulated private enterprise. (358)

Answers to the Self-Test

  I. 1. f; 2. d; 3. g; 4. a; 5. b; 6. i
 II. 1. d; 2. c; 3. f; 4. b; 5. i
III. 1. c; 2. b; 3. a; 4. a; 5. b; 6. b

CHAPTER 14

Attempts to Shape the American Character

The Historical Problem

This chapter explores why Americans in the early nineteenth century became so concerned with molding individual character. What were the sources of this concern with character formation? What forms did these campaigns for self-improvement take? What were the social consequences of the search for ways to shape the American character?

The Historical Problem Answered: The Chapter Thesis

Americans believed that the strength and vitality of their republican institutions depended on the moral character of the American people, and that that character was capable of being molded. This belief gave considerable social importance to those who promised ways to improve character — educators, religious revivalists, popular writers, phrenologists, and others.

Educational reformers, led by Horace Mann, argued that the public schools could preserve America's values, protect the continued existence of republican government, and prepare individuals to succeed in a competitive society. The influence of Protestant revivalism varied from region to region, but revivals seemed to counteract destructive individualism while acting as important socializing forces. A variety of fads and cults, ranging from spiritualism to phrenology, appealed to Americans because they offered a technology for control of the mind and for determination of character. Emerson became America's premier philosopher because he eloquently called for the constant reshaping of individual as well as American character.

American art, as it developed during these years, mastered the traditional techniques of European art but applied them to American themes and subjects. The need to sell artistic products in a commercial economy encouraged the cultivation of sentimentality and moralism.

The Chain of Arguments and Evidence

"We Must Educate or Perish"   TEXT PAGES

The Evangelical Age

The Cult of Self-Improvement

The Tensions of Democratic Art

People, Places, and Events

1. *Charles G. Finney* (1792-1875) was the most effective and influential revivalist of the early nineteenth century. Unlike earlier religious leaders, Finney was not academically trained for the ministry.
   He was a lawyer who experienced conversion and then turned his
   considerable talents to revival preaching. Licensed to preach as a
   Presbyterian, Finney was the center of the powerful revivals that
   swept through the "burned-over" district of western New York state
   after 1825. His supporters established the Broadway Tabernacle for
   him in New York City in 1834. His *Lectures on Revivals* (1835) is
   a defense of revivalism and a guidebook on how to have a revival.
   Finney argued that each person was able "to repent, to believe in
   Christ and to accept salvation." In one sense, Finney was the first
   modern revivalist because he acted on his conviction that revivals
   were not miracles; but rather that they were events created by revivalists to achieve spiritual results.

2. *Transcendentalists* were ardent, young, intellectual men and women
   who shared certain enthusiasms, attitudes, and commitments that did
   not form a consistent philosophy. The Transcendentalists were literary
   men and women, mainly New Englanders, who were influenced by
   the moral enthusiasm of their Puritan forebears and by the Romantic

movements in Germany and England. Some of these Americans gathered around Ralph Waldo Emerson and Bronson Alcott in Concord, Massachusetts.

If they had one thing in common, besides an interest in literature, it was the conviction that intuition, imagination, and faith were more important than science, reason, and materialism. *The Dial,* edited by Margaret Fuller, was published from 1840 to 1844 and was the Transcendentalist periodical. Other Transcendentalists were (at least for a time) Orestes Brownson, Henry David Thoreau, and Theodore Parker. The Transcendentalists called for Americans to recover their moral inheritance by recognizing the divine in human nature. They contributed decisively to the literary Renaissance that distinguished the early nineteenth century.

3. *Lyceums* were created to encourage adult education and self-improvement. The lyceum movement, so characteristic of early nineteenth-century American life, began when Millbury Lyceum No. 1 was established at Millbury, Connecticut. In 1831, the National American Lyceum was organized at New York, and by 1834 there were 3,000 lyceums in fifteen states. A lyceum would organize a program of speakers in a community, and the lecturers would be chosen for their ability to enlighten the audience. Emerson was a popular speaker on the lyceum circuit, and science was one of the most popular subjects. When a scientist lectured on chemistry in Boston, on one occasion, crowds packed the streets outside the lecture hall. The aim of lyceums was to uplift, not to entertain.

4. *Henry David Thoreau* (1817-1862) was one Transcendentalist, a native of the town of Concord, Massachusetts, where he lived nearly his whole life. After being graduated from Harvard in 1837, Thoreau taught school, worked in the family pencil-making business, and lived with Emerson for a time.

Thoreau's real life was the emotional and intellectual life of his mind, which he recorded in his journals and then transmuted into perhaps the best prose ever written by an American. Thoreau's style combined the sinewy grace of his classical education and the rough-hewn nativisms of rural New England. He passed beyond Emerson's ideas on nature and developed his highly individualistic method of using nature observation as a medium for the understanding of himself, mankind, and American society. His first published work, *A Week on the Concord and Merrimack Rivers* (1849), used a river boat trip as the center of his reflections and observations. Thoreau's most important work, *Walden* (1854), organized his nature observations and reflections around an account of his residence in a little cabin on the edge of Walden Pond near Concord. His writings founded a vital and enduring tradition of American nature writing that flourishes today.

During the Mexican-American War, Thoreau refused to pay his Massachusetts poll tax in protest against the proslavery aspects of the war. He spent only a night in jail, but he also wrote his powerful and persuasive essay "On Civil Disobedience." In this, he justified passive civil disobedience in situations where the commission or perpetuation of injustice has become enmeshed in the very machinery of government. His arguments have influenced many in the twentieth century, from Ghandi and the Indian independence movement to contemporary Americans and Europeans. Although usually thought of as a recluse because of his Walden Pond stay, Thoreau was quite sociable and enjoyed company as much as the play of wit. He spoke out publicly against slavery in the 1850s and admired John Brown.

5. *Edgar Allan Poe* (1809-1849) was one early nineteenth-century American writer who transcended the literary conventions of the day. Poe was born in Boston but reared in Richmond, Virginia, after being orphaned at the age of three. He attended the University of Virginia but soon left because of gambling debts. The next year his first volume, *Tamerlane and Other Poems* (1827), was published anonymously. Poe enlisted in the army and attended West Point but was thrown out for neglect of duty.

More of his poetry was published, but his first popular success came with the appearance of "A MS. Found in a Bottle" in a Baltimore periodical. A patron helped Poe join the staff of the *Southern Literary Messenger* which he wrote for and helped to edit. But he soon married and moved to New York where he supported himself by editing and writing. In 1840 "The Gold Bug" won a literary prize.

But Poe's personal problems began to close in on him. His wife Virginia died of tuberculosis, and his drinking and gambling became worse. He died after being found semiconscious in a Baltimore saloon. Poe is the creator of the modern detective story as well as the master of the Gothic short story, and he greatly influenced French symbolist poets.

Self-Test

I. Match each identifying statement with the appropriate name.

a. Charles Grandison Finney (373)
b. Henry David Thoreau (382)
c. Ralph Waldo Emerson (379)
d. Horace Mann (367)

e. Lyman Beecher (364)
f. James Fenimore Cooper (381)
g. Washington Irving (381)

1. _____ The leading Transcendentalist poet, essayist, and lecturer who sang the praises of individualism, self-reliance, and idealism.

2. _____ The most effective champion of the public school movement who argued that democracy depended on the public schools.

3. _____ Though lacking in formal seminary training, he became the most commanding and influential evangelist in the pre-Civil War period.

4. _____ Author of a series of "Leatherstocking Tales" that expressed a distinctly American experience with Indians, violence, and social relationships in the wilderness.

II. Circle the phrase that best completes each statement.

1. Among other things, the public school movement urged that schools would   (a) help children learn how to succeed in a competitive world,   (b) train a new generation in classical learning and philosophy,   (c) promote a new morality based on secular rather than Christian principles. (367)

2. One result of the spread of evangelicalism in the South was that (a) there were serious discussions of the contradiction between slavery and Christianity,   (b) the number of slave insurrections increased, (c) planters increasingly encouraged the conversion of their slaves. (371)

3. Evangelical revivalists of the early nineteenth century generally believed that a successful revival movement depended upon   (a) predestination,   (b) God alone,   (c) careful planning. (372)

4. In the Mid-West, the revivals tended to   (a) increase social distinctions by uniting the more ambitious members of a community, (b) create social turmoil as poorer people were attracted to them, (c) encourage a growing sense of social equality in most communities. (373)

5. A common feature of the early nineteenth-century fads, causes, cults, and nostrums was that they all offered   (a) self-knowledge, (b) salvation,   (c) distraction from real social problems like poverty. (376)

6. Phrenology claimed to be   (a) a new religion,   (b) a philosophy of life,   (c) a science of the mind. (377)

7. Popular American artists in the early nineteenth century tended to dwell on the theme of   (a) commercialism,   (b) sentimentality, (c) territorial expansion. (381)

8. In the early nineteenth century, American artists increasingly (a) ignored America in favor of European styles and subjects, (b) became less creative and more derivative,   (c) used conventional artistic forms to treat native American subjects. (381)

Answers to the Self-Test

I. 1. c; 2. d; 3. a; 4. f
II. 1. a; 2. c; 3. c; 4. a; 5. a; 6. c; 7. b; 8. c

CHAPTER 15

Dissent, Protest, and Reform

The Historical Problem

The problem is to understand the nature and consequences of early nineteenth-century American reform movements. What were the purposes
of reform? What characterized the reformers and the reform causes?
How did other Americans react to reform movements? What were the
consequences of the reform movements? What were the limits of dissent
in American society?

The Historical Problem Answered: The Chapter Thesis

In the early nineteenth century, the Northeast, and New England in particular, produced a host of reform crusades to rejuvenate the social order.
Virtually all of these reforms aimed at the establishment of moral government in order to counter chaos. These reform crusades expanded the
boundaries of American culture, and helped to modernize American
society by defending individual self-expression and opportunity. The
reforms aimed at improvements that would foster individual opportunity
and progress. At the same time, they sought to recover a simplicity and
unity that seemed to have been lost in material pursuits.

The Mormons and abolitionists provide extended illustrations of reform
pushed to the limits of tolerable dissent. Many Americans found Mormonism and abolitionism objectionable for a number of reasons. The
two movements, in different ways, were protests against the values of
a self-seeking society. The Benevolent Empire of reform organizations,
unlike the Mormons, set out to transform American society. Although
this battery of reforms did not solve any social problems, it did sweep

millions of Americans into an evangelical culture that united a belief in human perfectibility with the possibility of an Ameican millennium.

The problem of Negro slavery illustrated the limitations of the reform empire because of the obvious disparity between the problem and the proposed solution, colonization. The abolitionists, produced by the spread of evangelicalism and inspired by British reform example, asked whether the nation would continue to adapt itself to a social system founded in violence.

The Benevolent Empire and the abolitionist drive also helped to stimulate a feminist movement that led to an organized campaign to promote women's rights. Abolitionism, divided by the questions of nonresistance to violence and of the proper role of women in the movement, became increasingly more interested in the politics of slavery. Political antislavery gradually moved toward the position that slavery should be excluded from the western territories.

The Chain of Arguments and Evidence

People, Places, and Events

1. *The Oneida Community* was one of the most unusual and successful
   of the many utopian communities established in the United States
   in the early nineteenth century. John Humphrey Noyes founded
   Oneida after having been powerfully affected by the revivalism of
   Charles G. Finney. Noyes was a perfectionist — that is, he believed
   that it was possible for men and women to live lives of sinless perfec-
   tion. But the goal of Oneida, like the goal of so many of the utopian
   communities, was social rather than individual; Noyes hoped to demonstrate the feasibility and desirability of Christian social comunalism.

   The Oneida Community abolished all private relationships, including
   ownership of private property and the marriage contract. Members
   of the community joined in plural marriage which made every male
   member the husband of every female member and every female member the wife of every male member. Although this may sound like
   modern promiscuity under the veil of religion, the evidence suggests
   that, as the communitarians intended, this form of plural marriage
   decreased rather than increased the amount of sexual activity. There
   could be no sex act without the voluntary consent of both man (husband) and woman (wife). Thus women were freed from sexual bondage
   to the will of their husbands, and husbands were freed from the
   bondage of having unreasonable power over their wives.

   Such arrangements certainly made the Oneida Community the
   most radical of any in the period. Yet the community prospered,
   and it lasted much longer than most other experimental groups.
   This was partly because Noyes was a capable businessman and an
   inspiring leader.

2. *Brigham Young* (1801-1877) achieved the remarkable feat of being
   a major religious leader and the founder of a stunningly successful
   western settlement. Brigham Young was born in Vermont, but his
   family moved to western New York when he was an infant, and
   so Young grew up in the "burned-over district" that was the center
   of the Finney revivals. In 1832, he converted to Mormonism, the
   religious movement that was forming around Joseph Smith in that
   part of New York state. He moved to the Mormon colony at Kirt-
   land, Ohio, and became one of the Apostles who led the church.
   He helped to establish the Mormon's new settlement at Nauvoo,
   Illinois, where he succeeded Joseph Smith after the founder was
   murdered by a mob. He held the church together in the face of hostility and open persecution, and came to the conclusion that Mormons would have to found their own community far from the Gentiles
   (non-Mormons).

Brigham Young's practical intelligence and energy made a success of the Mormon migration that began in the winter of 1846. He directed the group effort that settled Deseret, as the Mormons called the valley of the Great Salt Lake. When the area was organized as the Utah Territory in 1850, Young was named territorial governor, a post he held until 1857. During this same period, he was also president of the Church of Jesus Christ of Latter-Day Saints. The relations between Utah and the national government were strained partly on account of the practice of polygamy which he sanctioned. It is not clear exactly how many wives Young had, since many were purely "spiritual wives" whom he never saw. He did father at least fifty-six children. Besides that, his major accomplishment was the construction of an administrative system that enabled the church to survive and develop.

3. *The American Colonization Society* was organized in 1817, the fruit of plans to move toward the elimination of slavery by aiding freed blacks to return to Africa. The assumption was that colonization would encourage slaveholders to free slaves whom they would not otherwise release. The society dispatched the first group of eighty-eight free blacks in 1820, and they settled on the coast of West Africa where they founded Liberia. The mathematics of population reproduction doomed the American Colonization Society's efforts because more slaves were born in a day than were (or could be) shipped to Africa in a year. Free blacks criticized the colonization movement on the ground that it was more obviously aimed at ridding America of free Negroes than at ridding America of slavery. The nation of Liberia thus founded was largely neglected by the United States. Many abolitionists arrived at their very different position on slavery after abandoning colonization.

4. *Elizabeth Cady Stanton* (1815-1902) became the central figure in the feminist movement of the nineteenth century. A native New Yorker, she was graduated from Troy Female Seminary in 1832. Like so many ardent young people of the day, she involved herself in the temperance movement and in antislavery.

   At the World's Anti-Slavery Convention in London in 1840, Elizabeth Cady Stanton and Lucretia Mott were among the women who were not allowed to participate because of their sex. From this point on, her energies were mainly devoted to the issue of women's rights. With Lucretia Mott, Elizabeth Cady Stanton called the first women's rights convention that met at Seneca Falls, New York, and adopted a "Declaration of Sentiments" which Stanton had drafted. The meeting also adopted a resolution calling for women's suffrage. She and

Susan B. Anthony began their long collaboration in the cause of women's rights in 1851. Elizabeth Cady Stanton served from 1869 to 1890 as president of the National Woman Suffrage Association, and she was a nationally known lyceum lecturer.

5. *Frederick Douglass* (1817-1895) was a former slave who became an abolitionist and, in his later life, United States consul general to Haiti. Douglass was born into slavery in Maryland where he spent his early life on several plantations and lived in Baltimore where he learned the trade of ship's caulker.

    In 1838, Douglass escaped from slavery and fled to New Bedford, Massachusetts. Three years later, he attended a meeting of the Massachusetts Anti-Slavery Society which so moved him that he became an active abolitionist. In this cause, he published his *Narrative of the Life of Frederick Douglass* (1845), an account of his life as a slave which is one of the classics of American slavery literature. A commanding presence on the platform and an effective speaker who could indict slavery with special authority, Douglass faced considerable danger on the abolitionist lecture circuit. He lectured on antislavery in Britain and collected enough money to purchase his own freedom. In 1847, he founded his own newspaper, *The North Star*. During the Civil War, Douglass spoke on behalf of emancipation and black enfranchisement, and helped to raise black troops for the Union army. He held a few minor government posts before being appointed consul general to Haiti.

Self-Test

I. Match each identifying statement with the appropriate name.

a. Elijah P. Lovejoy (401)
b. Joseph Smith, Jr. (386)
c. Brigham Young (388)
d. Elizabeth Cady Stanton (402)
e. William Lloyd Garrison (398-399)
f. Angelina Grimké (402-403)

g. Frederick Douglass (406)
h. John Humphrey Noyes (404)
i. Arthur Tappan (400)

1. _____ New England's leading abolitionist and founder of *The Liberator*; his ideas on pacifism later divided the movement.

2. _____ His murder in Alton, Illinois gave the abolitionists a martyr, but also forced them to face the issue of nonviolence.

3. _____ Founder and leader of the experimental community of Oneida which posed a radical alternative to the economic, sexual, and educational practices of American society.

4. _____ A remarkable leader and organizer, he headed the Mormon migration to the valley of the Great Salt Lake and the new "State of Deseret."

5. _____ A former slave, as a northern free black he became an active abolitionist who helped translate abstract images of slavery into concrete experience for Northerners.

6. _____ Together with her sister, she left their slaveholding father's plantation and became especially effective as a spokesperson for both abolitionism and women's rights.

II. Match each identifying statement with one of the items below.

a. communitarianism (404)   e. free soil (405)
b. perfectionism (396)   f. Sabbatarianism (394)
c. temperance (396)   g. polygamy (388)
d. colonization (397)   h. feminism (403-404)

1. _____ The most important spinoff from the abolitionist movement, it culminated in the Seneca Falls convention which demanded a broadening of the franchise.

2. _____ The most popular form of political abolitionism, it promised to exclude slavery from the western territories.

3. _____ A more conservative brand of antislavery, its advocates wanted the resettlement of blacks in Africa.

4. _____ A reaction against the crass commercialism of American life, it urged the use of boycotts to achieve its goal.

5. _____ A faith, both religious and secular, that individuals could be liberated from all coercive forces and institutions of society.

III. Circle the phrase that best completes each statement.

1. The Mormon movement provoked hostility and even violence because the Mormons   (a) wanted to spread slavery into areas where they settled,   (b) were so individualistic that they threatened to overturn public order,   (c) rejected the values of a highly competitive, uprooted society. (391)

2. The Benevolent Empire was   (a) the Antebellum South, where cotton was king,   (b) the unsettled territories of America's western frontier,   (c) a coalition of missionary and reform societies in Antebellum America. (391)

3. Abolitionists were distinguished from other antislavery groups in that they believed that   (a) slavery was the major national sin, (b) slaves should be helped to return to Africa,   (c) slavery should be abolished gradually and slaveowners fairly compensated. (398)

4. The abolitionists of the 1830s expected to accomplish their objectives by   (a) provoking violence,   (b) moral appeal,   (c) political organization. (398)

5. The national government responded to the abolitionists in the 1830s by   (a) debating the practicality of abolitionist petitions presented to Congress,   (b) prohibiting the circulation of abolitionist literature through the mails,   (c) banning slavery from the District of Columbia. (401)

6. Abolitionism gradually became more acceptable in the North partly by   (a) accommodating itself to white racism,   (b) adopting a more moralistic tone,   (c) emphasizing such other issues as pacificism. (406)

Answers to the Self-Test

I. 1. e; 2. a; 3. h; 4. c; 5. g; 6. f
II. 1. h; 2. e; 3. d; 4. f; 5. b
III. 1. c; 2. c; 3. a; 4. b; 5. b; 6. a

CHAPTER 16

Expansion and New Boundaries

The Historical Problem

The historical problem is to explain the economic and foreign policy developments that led ultimately to sectional conflict. What economic changes influenced life in the North? How did slavery affect life in the South? What foreign policies did the United States implement in the early nineteenth century? How was slavery linked to American expansionism? What were the causes and consequences of the Mexican War?

The Historical Problem Answered: The Chapter Thesis

During the 1840s, after a period of preparation going back to the 1820s, a new economic era began in the North. This impressive economic growth was fueled by the expansion of manufacturing and the factory system, railroad construction, and immigration. The South, whose economy was dependent on cotton and slavery, became more firmly committed than ever before to slavery's desirability. The South had become a "slave society."

Protection of slavery had long been one among many objectives of American foreign policy. The growth of an American "empire for liberty" paradoxically expanded an American empire for slavery. The nation's expansionist foreign policy was given an even more explicitly proslavery orientation in President Polk's interpretation of the Monroe Doctrine in association with the annexation of Texas in 1845. American expansionist policies, aiming at the acquisition of California, climaxed in the Mexican War. And American success in that war made the question of slavery's role in American life inescapable.

The Chain of Arguments and Evidence

People, Places, and Events

1. *John C. Calhoun* (1782-1850) was the intellectual and political leader
   of the extreme proslavery position until his death. Calhoun was born in
   South Carolina of Scotch-Irish ancestry and educated at Yale from
   which he was graduated in 1804. After studying law and being admitted to the South Carolina bar, he took up politics.

   From 1811 to 1817 he served in Congress where he supported the
   nationalistic War of 1812 and the activist legislation by the central
   government that followed the war. He served as secretary of war
   under President Monroe from 1817 to 1825 and was elected vice-
   president in 1824 under John Quincy Adams and in 1828 under
   Andrew Jackson. Resigning from the vice-presidency in 1832, he was
   sent to the United States Senate by South Carolina where he served
   until his death.

   In the late 1820s as South Carolina changed, Calhoun's nationalism
   began to give way to the states' rights positions that he refurbished.
   He openly defended slavery as a "positive good," and he tried to
   contrive constitutional means by which the southern slavery interests,
   a numerical minority, could protect themselves. His *South Carolina
   Exposition and Protest* (1828) defended the legitimacy of state nullification of federal legislation. Later, Calhoun's driving, logical mind
   arrived at the conclusion that the South could be safe only if there
   were two presidents, one from the North and one from the South,
   each armed with a veto. This was not a very satisfactory solution
   to the sectional conflict, and its unreality was made all the clearer
   by Calhoun's companion requirement for national peace and harmony,
   that the agitation of the slavery issue be ended. That could be accomplished, of course, only by the imposition of a police state.

Calhoun died before the sectional crisis exploded in the Civil War, but he had laid the constitutional foundations on which secession was based and justified. His political writings are of some interest today because of their logical force, clear reasoning, and concern with the defense of minority rights. But Calhoun was not interested in protecting the rights of all minorities; he devoted his intellectual powers to the protection of a minority of slaveholders.

2. *George Fitzhugh* (1806-1881) was, with John C. Calhoun, one of the ablest and most intellectually interesting defenders of slavery. Fitzhugh was born in Prince William County, Virginia and was self-educated. He practiced law, but was mainly a journalist who contributed to the *Richmond Enquirer* and *DeBow's Review*. His major contributions to the discussion of slavery were *Sociology for the South, or the Failure of Free Society* (1854) and *Cannibals All! or Slaves Without Masters* (1856).

Fitzhugh criticized any society based on the laissez-faire principle of free competition on the grounds that this merely legitimized exploitation. Free competition, he argued, would dehumanize children and women workers. For these reasons he found free society immoral because it had no place for Christian virtue, "that virtue which bids us love our neighbor as ourself. . . . " The solution for the problem of selfishness in society was to find a way "to identify the interests of the weak and the strong, the poor and the rich."

Slavery's valuable social function was that it accomplished that very thing. The dependence of slaves on their masters produced love. "A state of dependence," he wrote, "is the only condition in which reciprocal affection can exist among human beings." Consequently, the slaveholder, in contrast to the arguments of the abolitionists, was the highest order of moral man because he spent his life in providing for those dependent on him. Significantly, Fitzhugh's defense of slavery took the form of an incisive criticism of the North. He once admitted that he saw "great evils in slavery," but he never wrote about them.

3. *James K. Polk* (1795-1845) is considered by many to be the most successful president because he achieved all of the goals he espoused upon taking office. Polk was born in North Carolina, but his family moved to Tennessee when he was a boy. He was graduated from the University of North Carolina in 1818 and began the practice of law and politics in Tennessee.

After serving in the state legislature, he was elected to Congress where he sat from 1825 to 1839 and emerged as a Democratic leader of the House. After serving as governor of Tennessee from 1839-1841, he accepted the 1844 Democratic party nomination for president. Polk was a Jacksonian Democrat and an avid expansionist.

Upon taking office Polk promised to reduce tariffs, reestablish the independent treasury, settle the Oregon question with Britain, and promote westward expansion. The Walker Tariff (1846) reformed the tariff system and was based on the principle of raising revenue rather than providing protection. The independent treasury system, originally advocated by Martin Van Buren, was reestablished. Polk compromised with Britain on the Oregon question, but secured control over a large portion of the disputed region without resorting to war. In the Far West and Southwest, negotiations with Mexico proved fruitless, and Polk went to war to achieve his territorial goals. As a result of the Mexican-American War, Polk added more land area to the United States than any other president except Thomas Jefferson. Polk did not seek reelection. Perhaps, having accomplished what he set out to do in his first term, there was no point in serving another four years.

4. *The Ostend Manifesto* expressed the proslavery ambitions that influenced American foreign policy in the 1840s and 1850s. Spanish officials in Havana, Cuba seized and condemned an American vessel, an action that elicited calls for war in Congress. The secretary of state, William Marcy, instructed the American ministers to Spain, France, and Great Britain to meet at Ostend, Belgium to propose a policy for the acquisition of Cuba. They met on October 9, 1854, and the resulting report is the Ostend Manifesto.

The diplomats urged that the United States should make every effort to obtain Cuba in order to protect American slavery. They added economic arguments for that policy and feared that Spain would free all Cuban slaves who would then Africanize the island. If that happened, they continued, the United States would be justified in using force to take Cuba from Spain.

Although the paper was a confidential diplomatic dispatch to the secretary of state, it was made public, and the resulting clamor forced the secretary to disavow the contents of the Ostend Manifesto. It did not go away, however, for the aggressive proposals hung in the air as reminders of the strength and ambition of the Slave Power.

Self-Test

I. Match each identifying statement with the appropriate name.

a. George Fitzhugh (417)
b. John Quincy Adams (420, 422)

e. John C. Frémont (429)
f. Nicholas Trist (433)

c. John Slidell (429)   g. Zachary Taylor (430)
d. Thomas Hart Benton (426)   h. Sam Houston (423)

1. _____ The primary author of the Monroe Doctrine, he also negotiated the purchase of Florida and was one of America's
most successful secretaries of state.

2. _____ He negotiated the Treaty of Guadalupe Hidalgo with Mexico
even though his authority to do so had been withdrawn.

3. _____ Commander of American troops in Texas whose fortifications
on the Rio Grande provoked Mexico into war in 1846.

4. _____ Leader of the Texan army during their revolution against
the Mexican government in 1836.

5. _____ Author of *Cannibals All!* which argued that the South's
peculiar institution was far more humane and Christian than
the "wage slavery" of the North.

II. Circle the phrase that best completes each statement.

1. The American system of manufacturing depended on   (a) a plentiful supply of skilled labor,   (b) light machine tools that eliminated
many hand operations,   (c) secrets stolen from British and German
industry. (411)

2. Those who suffered least from the Panic of 1857 were   (a) southern
planters,   (b) railroad investors,   (c) northern manufacturers.
(415)

3. In the period between 1820 and 1860, the South was   (a) like the
rest of the country except that it was more rural and poorer,
(b) largely dominated by cotton plantations,   (c) a large and
regionally diversified section. (415)

4. The most dramatic growth of slavery by 1840 was in the   (a) western states,   (b) Gulf Coast states,   (c) Upper South. (416)

5. Southern proslavery advocates generally based their defense of that
institution on   (a) capitalism,   (b) liberalism,   (c) racism.
(417)

6. Major objectives of American foreign policy in the 1840s included
all of the following *except*   (a) the protection of slavery,
(b) an alliance with Great Britain,   (c) the acquisition of California. (417–418)

7. Most Americans who migrated to Oregon in the 1840s were (a) gold miners, (b) farmers, (c) fur trappers. (427)

8. The United States stated its opposition to European intervention in the Western Hemisphere in the (a) Transcontinental Treaty, (b) Webster-Ashburton Treaty, (c) Monroe Doctrine. (422)

9. A major battle of the Mexican War occurred at (a) Buena Vista, (b) San Jacinto, (c) the Alamo. (432)

10. The Ostend Manifesto would have had the United States acquire (a) all of Mexico, (b) Oregon to 54°40', (c) Cuba. (434)

Answers to the Self-Test

I. 1. b; 2. f; 3. g; 4. h; 5. a
II. 1. b; 2. a; 3. c; 4. b; 5. c; 6. b; 7. b; 8. c; 9. a; 10. c

CHAPTER 17

Compromise and Conflict

The Historical Problem

The problem is to understand how and why Americans' fear of unchecked power became focused on the conflict between free and slave states. How did slavery polarize American values? Why did a growing number of Northerners become convinced that slavery threatened the attainment of their social ideals? Why did Southerners fear the consequences of the withdrawal of federal protection of slavery? Why was the two-party system unable to resolve the sectional conflict over slavery? Why did slavery become an insoluble political issue after 1845? What caused the American Civil War? Why did southern states begin to secede in the winter of 1860–1861?

The Historical Problem Answered: The Chapter Thesis

During the years from 1820 to 1860, America seemed to have overcome boundaries of all kinds, and the American individual seemed to have attained unlimited freedom. But the question of Negro slavery became the critical issue on which the fears of unchecked power which also developed in Americans at that time was focused. Southerners felt that Northerners had abandoned their commitment to the national understanding that slavery would be protected. Northerners thought that freedom would endure only if slavery was set on the path to ultimate extinction. In national life, the question was fought out in connection with the disposition of the western territories, particularly those acquired in the Mexican War. Although the Compromise of 1850 suggested that political arts could handle the sectional disagreement over slavery, the slavery issue fractured the two-party system by destroying the more vulnerable Whig party. The revival of the slavery question in the Kansas-Nebraska Act and the appearance of a Republican party committed to the exclusion of slavery from the federal territories were signals of a growing sectional division. The outbreak of fighting in Kansas and the Lecompton Constitution split the Democratic party. The national political system had become a casualty of slavery. North and South tended to see each other as a conspiratorial power with which it was impossible to compromise; and Americans in both sections believed in standing up to tyrannical conspirators. With the Republican victory of 1860, South Carolina led the way into secession.

The Chain of Arguments and Evidence

People, Places, and Events

1. *Stephen A. Douglas* (1813-1861) was a Democratic party leader who
   was at the center of political disputes over slavery from the Compro-

mise of 1850 to the presidential election of 1860. Douglas was born in Vermont, but he moved to the Old Northwest and settled in Illinois where he read law, was admitted to the bar, and ventured into politics. He wisely invested in land in the Chicago area and became wealthy. At the same time, he rose rapidly to political leadership in the national Democratic party. After holding state offices, he was elected to two terms in the House of Representatives, from 1843 to 1847, where he supported expansionism and the war against Mexico. At the age of thirty-five, Douglas was elected to the United States Senate where he held a seat until his death.

In the political conflict between sections, Douglas was a compromiser, holding to the doctrine of popular sovereignty. This would allow the settlers in a territory to decide for themselves whether or not they wanted to allow slavery. It was Douglas who re-ignited the slavery issue in politics by introducing the Kansas-Nebraska Act in 1854. This act, incorporating the principle of popular sovereignty, repealed the Missouri Compromise. Douglas was willing to make this repeal explicit in the later stages of the bill's progress, because his presidential ambition needed the support of southern, proslavery Democrats. He did not win the Democratic presidential nomination in 1852 or in 1856.

Douglas finally broke with the proslavery Democrats when he denounced the Buchanan administration's violation of popular sovereignty in Kansas. His efforts to reconcile the *Dred Scott* decision with popular sovereignty during the Lincoln-Douglas debate further separated him from the southern wing of the party. When he finally won the party's nomination in 1860, the Democrats had fractured into sectional wings and there was no chance of winning the presidency. He opposed secession and appeared to be a strong unionist when he died of typhoid fever.

2. *The Fugitive Slave Act of 1850* was passed as part of the Compromise of 1850. It was a measure that proslavery forces wanted very badly, but its operation only harmed the cause the act was supposed to defend. The act amended the weak Fugitive Slave Act of 1793 and considerably strengthened the federal role in all cases involving fugitive slaves. It placed fugitive slave cases in federal jurisdiction and established special United States commissioners who were authorized to issue warrants for the arrest and return of runaway bondsmen. An affadavit by a claimant was considered adequate proof of ownership of a runaway. Blacks who claimed to be free were denied the right of trial by jury, and their testimony was not admitted as evidence in the hearing. Citizens who prevented the arrest of a fugi-

tive, who concealed a fugitive, or who did not aid in the capture of a fugitive when requested were subject to fine, imprisonment, and payment of civil damages.

Many Northerners were deeply offended by a bill which seemed to place the national government in the business of apprehending run-away slaves and which seemed to violate civil liberties. Its symbolic and psychological results were to damage the proslavery cause by outraging many Northerners. To make matters worse, the law's provisions were largely unenforceable.

3. *Harriet Beecher Stowe* (1811-1896) was one of the most effective antislavery propagandists. She was born in Litchfield, Connecticut, where her father Lyman Beecher was one of the leaders of New England evangelicalism. Her brother Henry Ward Beecher became perhaps the most famous and influential minister in mid-nineteenth-century America. She moved to Cincinnati when her father became president of Lane Theological Seminary. There, in 1836, she married Calvin Stowe, a professor of Biblical literature at the seminary. The Stowes later moved to Bowdoin College in Brunswick, Maine.

She had already imbibed antislavery views at Lane long before passage of the Fugitive Slave Act of 1850. Stunned by that measure, she began to write *Uncle Tom's Cabin, or Life Among the Lowly* which was published serially in an antislavery periodical, *National Era*, from June 1851 to April 1852. The book form of this novel sold more than 300,000 copies in a year and it became one of the most widely known novels in the English language. This may have been the most effective abolitionist writing of the whole campaign against slavery.

Unfortunately, the novel is talked about more than it is read. Much of the discussion of the book centers on its accuracy about slavery, which is not the central issue. Stowe succeeded in giving personalities to the slave characters, even though some are wooden; it would be difficult for a sensitive reader to think of slaves as abstractions after having read the novel. The novel's central theme is that slavery destroys the American family, black and white, and so must be eliminated before it shatters American society.

Harriet Beecher Stowe became a popular writer and some of her later works survive as well as *Uncle Tom's Cabin*. After the Civil War, she lived most of the remainder of her life in Florida.

4. *John Brown* (1800-1859) was the central symbolic figure of mid-nineteenth-century American life. He was born in Connecticut and was an unsuccessful businessman. Brown first emerged into public notice when he took part in the guerrilla war that burst out in Kansas

between pro- and antislavery forces. In 1856, Brown led a small party, including four of his own sons, that murdered five proslavery settlers at Pottawatomie Creek. Brown justified this act as retaliation for proslavery atrocities; proslavery leaders denounced the act as wanton murder, proof of abolitionist radicalism. Brown was now an open advocate for stronger action against slavery, a position that won him financial and moral support from some antislavery Northerners.

In October 1859, Brown led a party of nineteen, including five blacks, in a raid on the federal arsenal at Harpers Ferry, Virginia. Brown seems to have considered this to be the beginning of a slave revolt that he could then furnish with arms from the captured arsenal. But no slaves came to his support, and no insurrection took place. A military force of United States marines, commanded by Colonel Robert E. Lee, easily captured Brown and his band. At his trial for treason, he spoke with passion and perception about slavery's function in American life; Southerners saw him as the living proof of abolitionist madness. He was convicted and hanged in December 1859. The Civil War certified his martyrdom.

Map Exercise

Limiting the Spread of Slavery

The spread of slavery was affected by the following acts: (a) the Missouri Compromise of 1820;   (b) the Compromise of 1850;   (c) the Kansas-Nebraska Act of 1854. Review the text discussion of the Missouri Compromise in Chapter 13; the Compromise of 1850 and the Kansas-Nebraska Act in Chapter 17, and the maps on pp. 343, 444, and 449 in the text.

1. On the appropriate maps on pp. 274, 275, and 276 at the back of this Student Guide, shade in the areas that were either slave states or slave territories, or were open to slavery under each of these acts. In the case of the Missouri Compromise, indicate the dividing line between slave and free territory.

Self-Test

I. Match each identifying statement with the appropriate name.

   a. David Wilmot (439)   e. Roger B. Taney (451)
   b. Henry Clay (442)   f. John C. Calhoun (439, 443)
   c. Charles Sumner (450)   g. William Seward (443)
   d. Stephen Douglas (447)   h. John Brown (456)

1. _____ An antislavery senator who was bodily beaten in the Senate chamber in an incident that demonstrated to many Northerners that a slave society bred violence.

2. _____ Argued during the debate on the Compromise of 1850 that the Union could be preserved only if the South were guaranteed a way to protect itself from a hostile federal government.

3. _____ Pennsylvania congressman whose attempt to bar slavery from the Mexican Cession Territory stimulated the discussions leading to the Compromise of 1850.

4. _____ Author of the Kansas-Nebraska bill who became the foremost proponent of "popular sovereignty" in the 1850s.

5. _____ Chief Justice of the Supreme Court who wrote the majority decision in the *Dred Scott* case.

II. Circle the phrase that best completes each statement.

1. The Compromise of 1850 included all of the following *except* (a) passage of a more stringent Fugitive Slave Act, (b) repeal of the Missouri Compromise, (c) admission of California as a free state. (443)

2. Harriet Beecher Stowe's *Uncle Tom's Cabin* was aimed at the horrifying implications of (a) popular sovereignty, (b) the Fugitive Slave Act, (c) the *Dred Scott* decision. (444)

3. The massive immigration of Irish and Germans in the period 1845–1854 stimulated (a) the movement of slaves to the deep Southwest, (b) the repeal of the Missouri Compromise, (c) an upsurge of political nativism. (446)

4. "Bleeding Kansas" is important because, among other things, it (a) united the Democratic party, (b) demonstrated the limitations of popular sovereignty as a solution to the slave issue, (c) changed abolitionism into a radical movement committed to violence. (448–449)

5. During the Kansas crisis, the Lecompton constitution was endorsed by (a) President Buchanan, (b) Senator Stephen Douglas, (c) the Republican party. (450)

6. In the Lincoln-Douglas debates, Lincoln criticized Douglas (a) for being a partisan Democrat, (b) for being morally indifferent to slavery, (c) for wanting to provoke a sectional war over slavery. (453)

7. One peculiarity of Lincoln's victory in 1860 was that   (a) he had broad support from all political parties,   (b) he won a majority of the popular vote despite being relatively unknown,   (c) he won not a single popular vote in ten of the slave states. (459)

8. From the South's point of view, the danger from the election of Lincoln sprang from the fact that   (a) the Republicans were committed to the abolition of slavery,   (b) his administration would be committed to the proposition that slavery was morally wrong,   (c) the Republicans now controlled the Senate, the House, and the presidency. (459)

Answers to the Self-Test

I. 1. c; 2. f; 3. a; 4. d; 5. e
II. 1. b; 2. b; 3. c; 4. b; 5. a; 6. b; 7. c; 8. b

PART FOUR

David Herbert Donald *Uniting the Republic*

1860–1877

Thesis

At the beginning of the Civil War, appearances suggested that the North
and the South formed two different nations with separate value systems
and moral codes. But the conduct of the war demonstrates that Union
and Confederacy were two parts of a cultural whole. The opposing sides
used similar approaches to the organization of their societies for war, and
they implemented similar military, manpower, and economic policies. By
the end of the Civil War, the two governments even committed themselves
to ending slavery, the most divisive of all the sectional issues. Postwar
events confirmed the cultural unity of the American people. Northerners
and Southerners shared the same assumptions about limited government,
economic laissez-faire, and white superiority, beliefs that limited the
innovations of the Reconstruction period.

The Civil War was a struggle within American society to find a balance
between nationalism and localism, between majority rule and minority
rights. In the war and its aftermath Americans found a new compromise
solution, a moderate and practical balance between nationalism and localism.

Chronology

1861	Firing on Fort Sumter begins Civil War
1862	Battle of Antietam; preliminary Emancipation Proclamation issued
1863	Battle of Gettysburg; surrender of Vicksburg
1864	Battle of the Wilderness; Sherman marches through Georgia
1865	Thirteenth Amendment submitted for ratification; Lee surrenders; Lincoln assassinated
1866	Fourteenth Amendment proposed
1867	Military Reconstruction Acts passed
1870	Fifteenth Amendment adopted
1873-1879	Depression
1876-1877	Compromise of 1876-1877 settles the disputed election
1890	Beginning of final disfranchisement of blacks in southern states

CHAPTER 18

Stalemate, 1861–1862

The Historical Problem

The problem is to understand the similarities and differences between the Union and the Confederacy during the first two years of war. How did the Union and Confederate governments organize themselves? What financial, diplomatic, and military policies did each follow? What does their conduct of the war tell us about the similarities and differences between North and South? What explains the stalemated war in 1861 and 1862?

The Historical Problem Answered: The Chapter Thesis

The aims of the hostile governments were certainly incompatible, but the organization and actions of both the Union and the Confederacy during 1861 and 1862 demonstrated clearly that the American people formed one nation rather than two. The government of the Confederate States of America virtually duplicated the government of the United States. Both presidents struggled to form viable administrations in the midst of disorganization. Once their governments were in operation, the two leaders confronted similar problems in diplomacy, economics, and mobilization. They responded to their difficulties by moving along parallel lines. The military leaders of both armies had been trained by the same precepts at the same school, West Point. Because both sets of leaders applied the principles of Jomini to warfare, it was not possible for the North to apply its superior economic and numerical resources to achieve victory. The Battle of Antietam demonstrated that a war fought by such principles would end inconclusively, unless one or the other side moved in some new direction.

The Chain of Arguments and Evidence

People, Places, and Events

1. *Jefferson Davis* (1808-1889) faced an extremely difficult task in trying to lead the Confederacy during the Civil War. Davis was born in Kentucky, but he grew up in Mississippi. He was graduated from West Point (1828) and served as an army officer until 1835 when he resigned to become a planter in Mississippi. A slaveholder, Jefferson Davis also became a spokesman for the South and slavery, defending the region and the institution against the criticisms of abolitionists. He entered politics and served first in the House of Representatives, then in the United States Senate from 1847 to 1851. He did not support the Compromise of 1850 while a senator.

His West Point education, service in the Black Hawk War (1830–1831), and command of the Mississippi Rifles in the Mexican-American War (1845-1846) prepared him to serve effectively as secretary of war from 1853 to 1857 under President Pierce. As secretary of war, he strengthened the army and coastal defenses, and oversaw the surveys for a transcontinental railroad by the southern route. He also encouraged the president to sign the Kansas-Nebraska Act. He was elected to the United States Senate after his cabinet service, but he resigned when Mississippi seceded from the Union.

Although he was not the most ardent supporter of secession, Davis was chosen as the president of the Confederate States of America. Critics, both contemporaries and historians, have charged that Davis was an inept administrator and an uninspiring leader; he is accused of failing to delegate responsibility and of interfering in military operations. Others point out that he faced insuperable obstacles in attempting to create a government and a nation while fighting a war against an enemy superior in numbers and resources.

After the Confederacy collapsed, Davis was captured and imprisoned at Fort Monroe, Virginia from 1865 to 1867 when he was released on bail after having been indicted for treason. But the charges were dropped, and he was never tried. He later wrote his *Rise and Fall of the Confederate Government* (1881) and lived in retirement at the beautiful plantation, Beauvoir, on the Mississippi Gulf Coast.

2. *William H. Seward* (1801-1872) was Lincoln's secretary of state. Seward was born in upstate New York, educated at Union College (1820), and admitted to the New York bar. He became active in politics, first with the Anti-Masonic party and then as a Whig. With the help of Thurlow Weed, Seward was elected to two terms as governor of New York and then to the United States Senate.

Seward emerged as the leading antislavery politician in national life. During the arrangement of the Compromise of 1850, Seward opposed slavery on the grounds that there was a "higher law" than the Constitution. Because he was the most widely known antislavery political leader, Seward expected to receive the nomination of the Republican party in 1860. But Lincoln was chosen, partly because he was considered more moderate on the slavery question than Seward who was associated with the abolitionist cause.

Lincoln did select Seward for his cabinet as secretary of state. During the secession crisis, Seward puzzled Lincoln and others by appearing to favor compromise with the South and by suggesting that the United States solve its domestic problems by provoking a foreign war. But Seward served effectively after that odd beginning.

His large views of the United States' future in the Pacific area influenced later generations of foreign-policy makers. He implemented his ideas spectacularly by acquiring Alaska. He also favored the acquisition of the Hawaiian Islands. At the time of Lincoln's assassination, Seward was wounded by one of John Wilkes Booth's co-conspirators, but he recovered to remain in the cabinet under President Andrew Johnson.

3. *"Stonewall" Jackson* (1824-1863) was one of the most colorful and tactically successful Confederate generals during the early stages of the Civil War. Jackson's real first name was Thomas, and he was born in western Virginia. After being graduated from West Point in 1846 and serving in the army during the Mexican-American War, Jackson became an instructor at the Virginia Military Institute in Lexington and resigned from the army in 1852.

    When the Civil War began, Jackson was commissioned as a brigadier general and won his famous nickname at the First Battle of Bull Run. His conduct of a campaign in the Shenandoah valley in the spring of 1862 was a dazzling success based on speed of movement, surprise, and aggressiveness. Then a major general, Jackson commanded units in other major engagements of the war. At the Second Battle of Bull Run, he led a daring flanking movement. During the Battle of Chancellorsville, Jackson was accidentally fired on by his own troops and was wounded. His death from pneumonia followed, depriving the Confederate armies of an unusually bold field commander.

4. *George B. McClellan* (1826-1885) was a Union general of great promise who disappointed his admirers and supporters. McClellan was graduated from West Point (1842) but, like so many officers of his generation, he resigned from the army in 1857. When war broke out in 1861, McClellan was commissioned as a major general in the Union army. His first success came in western Virginia which he secured in the early summer of 1861. Made general in chief of the Union army, he effectively organized, equipped, and trained the forces.

    Unfortunately, McClellan then undertook to attack Richmond up the peninsula between the York and James rivers. He compounded the disadvantages of this poor line of approach by moving with painful slowness. Lee succeeded in checking the Union push, and McClellan was forced to abandon his campaign. Lincoln then relieved McClellan of command, but gave it back to him when Lee invaded Maryland. During the Antietam campaign, McClellan again moved so cautiously that he apparently missed opportunities to win decisively. But in the climactic battle he at least achieved a draw with Lee. So slow was he to pursue Lee that Lincoln again relieved him of command, this time for the duration of the war.

The Democratic party nominated McClellan for president, and he ran against Lincoln in 1864. During the campaign, McClellan did not accept the Democratic party's plank calling for an immediate end to hostilities. Lincoln won and McClellan's political career was later fulfilled when he served as governor of New Jersey. McClellan is a good example of a military commander whose abilities did not suit him for battlefield command; they did make him an excellent organizer and trainer.

5. *Antietam (Sharpsburg)* is in western Maryland, north of the junction of the Shenandoah and Potomac rivers. Here, on September 17, 1862, Union and Confederate armies clashed in the climactic battle of Lee's first invasion of Maryland. McClellan pursued Lee, and there were preliminary battles at South Mountain and Harper's Ferry. When the main armies (70,000 Union and 40,000 Confederate) met near Sharpsburg, the fighting was so intense that each side suffered over 11,000 killed and wounded. Lee withdrew across the Potomac, giving at least the appearance of a Union victory. This enabled Lincoln to issue the preliminary Emancipation Proclamation.

Self-Test

I. Match each identifying statement with the appropriate name.

a. Ulysses S. Grant (488)   e. Edwin Stanton (478)
b. Salmon P. Chase (480)   f. Henry Halleck (488)
c. William Seward (482)   g. George McClellan (488–
d. Christopher Memminger (482)   489)

1. _____ Lincoln's secretary of war who eliminated much of the graft and inefficiency in that department and made the Union army the best supplied in the world.

2. _____ The Union general who first captured Forts Henry and Donelson in the West and later dominated the Eastern theater of military operations.

3. _____ Lincoln's cabinet officer who recommended that the secession crisis be dealt with by provoking a war with some European country.

4. _____ The Confederate secretary of treasury who, against his own wishes, but like his Union counterpart, was forced to use paper currency in order to finance the war effort.

5. _____ The Union commander who demonstrated skill at organizing and training an army, but who was reticent about leading it into battle during the Peninsular Campaign against Richmond.

II. Circle the phrase that best completes each statement.

1. In his inaugural address in 1861, President Lincoln vowed to (a) end slavery, (b) preserve the Union, (c) invade the South with Union armies. (470)

2. Both Lincoln and Davis's cabinets contained men who were (a) extremists, (b) incompetent, (c) close personal friends. (470)

3. The vital border state that Lincoln managed to hold in the Union after the firing on Ft. Sumter was (a) Virginia, (b) Tennessee, (c) Kentucky. (474)

4. The problem of the border states caused Lincoln to be cautious about (a) sending Union armies into the South, (b) imposing a naval blockade on the Confederacy, (c) the emancipation of slaves. (476)

5. Between 1861 and 1863, neither the Union nor the Confederacy enrolled for military service (a) volunteers, (b) conscripts, (c) blacks. (477–479)

6. Southern hopes for victory in the Civil War were heavily dependent upon (a) foreign aid, (b) naval supremacy, (c) taking the offensive. (483)

7. European nations based their policies toward the American Civil War on (a) national self-interest, (b) moral revulsion toward slavery, (c) their economic dependence on Southern cotton. (484)

8. Military commanders in both the North and the South initially employed the military theories that had been elaborated by (a) Robert E. Lee, (b) George McClellan, (c) Henri Jomini. (486)

9. It became clear that conventional rules of warfare would have to be modified after the indecisive battle of (a) Antietam, (b) Bull Run, (c) Gettysburg. (491)

Answers to the Self-Test

I. 1. e; 2. a; 3. c; 4. d; 5. g
II. 1. b; 2. b; 3. c; 4. c; 5. c; 6. a; 7. a; 8. c; 9. a

CHAPTER 19

Experimentation,
1862–1865

The Historical Problem

The problem is to understand the reasons for and the extent of political, social, economic, and military innovation by both the North and the South during the Civil War. When and why did they adopt novel approaches to their problems? Did they differ in their willingness to innovate? How did their experiments affect the Union, the Confederacy, and the outcome of the war? What do these innovations reveal about the cultural similarities and differences between the North and the South?

The Historical Problem Answered: The Chapter Thesis

The stalemate of the first two years of war forced both the Union and the Confederacy to adopt new political strategies, new forms of social and economic organization, and new ways of waging war. Both sides were original by the standards of the day, and the similarity of their creativity in war-making underlined their cultural unity. Military reality forced Union and Confederate soldiers to alter conventional tactics and abandon the infantry assault for entrenchments. Both sides strengthened their command systems as well. Compelled by necessity, the South was especially original in its approaches to naval warfare, but the Union blockade, made possible by the greater resources of the North, tightened ever more closely around the Confederacy. The war did not accelerate economic growth, but it did affect the structure of the economy and accustomed Northerners and Southerners to greater governmental activity in the economy.

Conscription caused resentment on both sides of the battle lines, and manpower needs compelled the governments to consider the use of blacks as soldiers. The Lincoln administration did this with the Emancipation Proclamation, and black soldiers established an excellent battle record. The Davis administration understandably moved more slowly in this same direction, but the war ended before black soldiers served in Confederate gray.

Opposition to the two leaders built up as the war dragged on, but military success saved the Lincoln administration. Slowly the Union had been able to mobilize the North's superior resources, while the South's scantier resources were used up. The absence of a political party system in the Confederacy had fatally weakened Davis's government, while the competitive politics of the Union had provided Lincoln with the conditions that made creative leadership possible and effective.

The Chain of Arguments and Evidence

Evolution of a Command System   TEXT PAGES

1. What conditions made Jomini's tactical theories invalid
   in the Civil War?   493-494
2. In what specific ways did the Northern and Southern
   armies abandon traditional military practices?   494
3. Why did Lincoln personally assume direction of Union
   military operations?   494
   a. How successful was he?   494-495
4. What was the significance of Grant's Vicksburg campaign?   495-496
5. How did Lincoln finally solve the command problem?   496
6. What was Grant's military strategy?   496-497
7. How did the Confederacy reorganize its military command?   497
   a. How well did the new system operate?   497

The Naval War

1. Why did the Confederacy take the lead in innovative
   approaches to naval warfare?   497-498
   a. What new weapons did the South develop?   498-499
2. What made the Union blockade effective?   499-500

The Wartime Economy

1. How did the war affect agriculture and industry in the
   North and the South?   500

People, Places, and Events

1. *Ulysses S. Grant* (1822-1885) was the most successful and most
   interesting Union general. Grant was born in Ohio and was graduated
   from West Point in 1843. He served during the Mexican-American
   War and was commended for gallantry at the Battle of Chapultepec.
   In 1854, he too resigned his commission and engaged in various occu-
   pations during the next several years. When war broke out, Grant
   was first made a colonel of the Illinois Volunteers, but was soon
   promoted. His capture of Forts Henry and Donelson established
   a well-earned military reputation that led to higher commands.

After surviving the near-disaster at Shiloh, Grant's first great success came with his unorthodox campaign to take Vicksburg. Lincoln gave Grant the supreme command of Union forces, and it was his leadership and strategy that won the final Union victories. While Grant held Lee in front of Richmond, Sherman's army drove from Chattanooga to Atlanta and on to the sea.

Grant has been criticized for accepting excessive casualties in a war of attrition. But the statistics for battle casualties do not bear out this charge. Grant was an offensive general, and the offense always takes more casualties; yet Grant's killed and wounded ratios do not seem to bear out the suggestion often heard that Grant was simply a "butcher" who overwhelmed the outnumbered Confederates with sheer weight of numbers. On the contrary, his Vicksburg campaign was brilliant, and the final strategic conception that led to Union victory was perfectly sound.

As a Union war hero, perhaps it was inevitable that Grant was elected president for two terms. After the White House, he toured the world and fell into financial difficulties. In a final act of great courage, this soldier's soldier while dying from cancer struggled to complete his *Personal Memoirs* in order to assure the financial security of his family.

2. *"Contrabands"* were escaped slaves who found their way across the military lines to seek sanctuary with Union forces. Union army commanders, seeking some legal device which would justify their provision of refuge for these runaway slaves, declared that they were "contraband of war" and so not legally returnable to their owners. The term "contraband of war" was first used by General Benjamin F. Butler when he commanded Fortress Monroe in Virginia. Although military commanders were supposed to return these fugitives during the initial stages of the war, the Second Confiscation Act (1862) freed slaves of those who committed treason or supported the rebellion. This and the later Emancipation Proclamation in effect assured that the contrabands would remain free. The term "contrabands" became a code word for escaped slaves.

3. *William T. Sherman* (1820-1891) has been called the first modern soldier by some authorities. His early career followed the pattern of so many others of his generation. Sherman was born and raised in Ohio and was graduated from West Point in 1840. After serving during the Mexican-American War, Sherman resigned his commission in 1855. After some other ventures, he was superintendent of a military academy at Alexandria, Louisiana from 1859 to 1861.

When the Civil War started, Sherman was given command of a regular army brigade, which he led at the First Battle of Bull Run. His emergence as a superb field commander began when he led a corps under Grant in the Vicksburg campaign; he thus became Grant's right arm. One military analyst has suggested that Sherman discovered the principles that lay behind Grant's military practice. In any case, the two formed an incomparable pair of commanders whether on the same battlefield or in the same theater of operations.

In the spring of 1864, Sherman was given control of the Western Union armies, and he immediately forced the Confederates to withdraw from Atlanta. Then Sherman abandoned his base of supplies, set out with 60,000 men, and drove through the Confederacy toward Savannah before turning North through the Carolinas. Nothing could have been further removed from the principles of Jomini. Yet this was the decisive military action in combination with Grant's push toward Richmond. The campaign also reflected a modern awareness of the economic and psychological dimensions of war. After the Civil War, Sherman held the post of general in chief of the army for fourteen years. He steadfastly refused the blandishments of politics.

4. *Joseph E. Johnston* (1807-1891) was one of the better Confederate commanders, but he had the ill luck to be matched against Sherman in the later phases of the war. Johnston was born in Virginia and educated at West Point from which he was graduated in 1829. During the Mexican-American War, he was wounded five times. Unlike his contemporaries, Johnston remained in the army and rose to the rank of brigadier general in 1860.

When Virginia seceded, Johnston did too, and he was commissioned as a brigadier general in the Confederate army in May 1861. He was one of the Confederate commanders at the First Battle of Bull Run, and he later led the forces defending Richmond during the initial stages of the peninsula campaign. Lee replaced Johnston when the latter was wounded. Later Johnston was the commander facing Sherman between Chattanooga and Atlanta. When he fell back before Sherman's maneuvering forces, Johnston was relieved of his command, although it is difficult to see what he could have done under the circumstances. This was one source of conflict within the Confederate government, as the Congress asked for Johnston's reinstatement. He commanded the army of Tennessee in the Carolinas during the last campaign of the war and surrendered to Sherman near Durham Station, North Carolina in April 1865. Johnston refused Jefferson Davis's order to continue fighting in the interior.

In postwar years, Johnston became a businessman, served in Congress (1879–1881), and in 1885 the old rebel soldier was appointed a Federal railroad commissioner.

5. *The Morrill Act,* passed in 1862, accomplished the objectives of Westerners who had long supported government assistance for technical and agricultural education. Under provisions of the act, each state was given 30,000 acres for each representative and senator in order to support higher education in the field of agriculture. Some states used the land grants to support existing schools, while others created new colleges. More than 13 million acres of land have been distributed under provisions of the act and later amendments; about seventy colleges were founded with this assistance. These so-called land-grant colleges have contributed enormously to public higher education, particularly in the Midwest and Far West.

Map Exercise

Major Civil War Battles

1. On the map on p. 277 at the back of this Student Guide, locate the following significant places:

Montgomery	New Orleans	Savannah	Atlanta
Richmond	Charleston	Washington, D.C.	

2. With the help of the text maps on pp. 487, 488, 495, 496, 517 and 518, (a) locate the following important battles on the Student Guide map:

Shiloh	Vicksburg	Appomattox
Fort Donelson/Fort Henry	Gettysburg	
Bull Run	The Wilderness	

(b) Then, using arrows of two different colors, indicate the direction of these two campaigns: Peninsula Campaign; Sherman's March to the Sea.

3. The shaded areas on the map indicate the areas in the South that fell under Union control at several points in the Civil War. Identify the area that was under Union control   (a) at the outbreak of the war, (b) by mid-1862,   (c) by mid-1863,   (d) by 1864.

Self-Test

I. Match each identifying statement with the appropriate name.

a. Frederick Douglass (506)	e. George Meade (517)
b. William T. Sherman (518)	f. Benjamin Wade (516)

c. Edmund Kirby-Smith (497)   g. Alexander Stephens (512)
d. Gideon Welles (499)   h. Robert E. Lee (494)

1. _____ The Radical Republican senator who attempted to establish Congress's authority to design reconstruction policy at the end of the Civil War; Lincoln vetoed his proposal.

2. _____ Confederate president Jefferson Davis's vice-president and one of his severist critics; he charged that Davis was trying to make himself a dictator.

3. _____ The Union general who assisted with Grant's victory at Vicksburg, captured Atlanta, and marched through Georgia to capture Savannah.

4. _____ A free black spokesman in the North who urged Lincoln to enroll blacks for military service in the Union army.

5. _____ The Confederate commander of the trans-Mississippi region in the western Confederacy.

II. Circle the phrase that best completes each statement.

1. As early as 1862, Congress was freeing slaves by ordering military commanders not to return   (a) "copperheads,"   (b) "contrabands,"   (c) conscripts. (507)

2. Innovation in naval warfare was most marked   (a) in the Union, which had a stronger naval tradition,   (b) in the Confederacy, which had better shipbuilding facilities,   (c) in the Confederacy, because necessity is the mother of invention. (498)

3. An important economic effect of the Civil War was that it (a) stimulated a dramatic growth of the overall national economy, (b) introduced government ownership of basic industries,   (c) provoked industrial expansion in both the North and the South. (500)

4. In order to finance the war, both Union and Confederate governments used all of the following methods *except*   (a) bond sales, (b) paper money issues,   (c) loans from foreign governments. (500)

5. Even before the Emancipation Proclamation, Congress abolished slavery in   (a) Washington, D.C.,   (b) the border states, (c) states that were at the time in rebellion against the government of the United States. (507)

6. Among its other consequences, the Emancipation Proclamation (a) ended slavery, (b) convinced European nations that the Union cause was also an antislavery cause, (c) united the North behind the Lincoln administration. (510)

7. Abraham Lincoln was criticized during the Civil War for doing all of the following *except* (a) issuing the Emancipation Proclamation, (b) violating constitutionally guaranteed civil liberties, (c) ignoring party politics and political considerations. (513)

8. Perhaps the fatal weakness of the Confederacy was that it lacked (a) a political party system, (b) enough capable generals, (c) effective civilian leadership. (520)

Answers to the Self-Test

I. 1. f; 2. g; 3. b; 4. a; 5. c
II. 1. b; 2. c; 3. c; 4. c; 5. a; 6. b; 7. c; 8. a

CHAPTER 20

Reconstruction, 1865–1877

The Historical Problem

The problem is to understand and explain the Civil War settlement. How were the seceded states treated by the victorious North? What provisions were made for the freedmen? Why did Reconstruction take the form that it did in 1865–1869? What was the Civil War settlement, and how was it achieved? What were the consequences of the settlement for the freedmen, for the South, and for the whole nation?

The Historical Problem Answered: The Chapter Thesis

The Civil War ended slavery and secession, but the war left unresolved the question of how the seceded states would be treated and the problem of the future status and political rights of the freed slaves. The first efforts to handle the problems of Reconstruction were made by President Lincoln and his successor, Andrew Johnson.

After first trying to cooperate with presidential Reconstruction, congressional Republicans swept aside Johnson's policies and implemented their own Reconstruction program. This gave the rights of citizenship to the freedmen and reorganized the former Confederate states under governments with new constitutions that provided for Negro suffrage. The Southern states were readmitted to the Union when this had been done, and they were controlled by Republican governments that depended on Negro votes.

Although this is called Radical Reconstruction, the name is misleading. Several factors seriously limited the amount of change that Americans even contemplated. Americans' beliefs in limited government, economic laissez-faire, and the racial superiority of whites narrowed the range of Reconstruction actions that were considered. In addition, the political parties, especially the division between Radical and Moderate (or Conservative) Republicans, tempered the extremes. Because actual programs had to meet the approval of a variety of factions, they tended to be moderate. In fact, the actual Reconstruction program owed more to the Moderate Republicans than to the Radicals. The dominant racism of white Americans also limited their approaches to the problem of defining a new status for the freedmen. The racism of Southern whites guaranteed their bitter hostility to Reconstruction and to the state governments created by the Republicans.

After President Grant let Southern whites know that, although open violence would not be tolerated, his administration would not interfere with less extreme measures, native white Redeemers toppled Republican state governments across the South. The set of agreements that resolved the disputed election of 1876 kept the presidency in Republican hands and assured the Redeemers that the central government would not interfere with them in the South. Once in control, the Redeemers moved to limit and then to exclude blacks from participation in politics. The new American compromise did not include blacks.

The Chain of Arguments and Evidence

Racism as a Limit to Change

The Restoration of "Home Rule"

People, Places, and Events

1. *Andrew Johnson* (1808-1875) was a Southern Democrat who became president in a Northern Republican administration; the results were predictable. Johnson was born in North Carolina and he moved to Tennessee as a youth. He was a self-educated, hard-working tailor whose ambition led him into politics. A Jacksonian Democrat, Johnson was elected to the state legislature and then to a House seat, the governorship of Tennessee (1853-1857), and the United States Senate (1857-1862).

   In personal life as in politics, Johnson represented the non-slave-owning white farmers and workers of the upper South. Yet he also opposed the abolitionist movement. When the secession crisis developed, Johnson was the highest ranking (United States senator) Southern politician to support the Union cause, even though Tennessee seceded. Johnson was selected to be Lincoln's vice-presidential running mate in 1864 in order to offer a bipartisan Union ticket.

   When he became president, Johnson's incapacities for that demanding position became clear. Under the circumstances, it would have been trying for even the most skillful leader, but Johnson's poor judgment and inability to control his temper hastened the split between the president and the Republican-controlled Congress. Johnson opposed the congressional Republicans' approach to Reconstruction, but he had no alternatives of his own that would have been satisfactory to the majority of Northerners in the aftermath of a bitter Civil War. Unable or unwilling to win support in Congress, Johnson lost the opportunity to govern, and the Republicans simply passed the major Reconstruction acts over his veto.

   His impeachment and subsequent trial demonstrated how completely the national Union administration had disintegrated. Returning to Tennessee after his unhappy and unsuccessful presidential years, Johnson was elected to the U.S. Senate in 1874, but he died the next year.

2. *Thaddeus Stevens* (1792-1868) was one of the leading Radical Republicans during the Reconstruction period. Stevens was born in Vermont, graduated from Dartmouth College in 1814, and then moved to Pennsylvania where he became a lawyer and involved himself in the iron industry. In politics, he moved from Anti-Masonry through the Whig party to the new Republican party. He had earlier become a convert to antislavery and, as a lawyer, had defended fugitive slaves. He was elected to the House of Representatives as a Republican from 1858 until his death.

   In Congress, Stevens became chairman of the Ways and Means Committee and supported strong measures to bring the South into line with Northern ideas of nationalism and to protect the rights of the freed slaves. Stevens despised the slaveowners and plantation elite who had led the secession movement and who had directed the South during the war. His name became synonymous with harsh vindictiveness, although it might as easily have been associated with concern for the blacks who were the victims of slavery. He helped to pass the Freedmen's Bureau Bill and Civil Rights Act over Johnson's vetos. He was a member of the Joint Congressional Committee on Reconstruction that drafted the Fourteenth Amendment and prepared the way for the passage of the Reconstruction Acts of 1867. He was also a prime mover behind the impeachment of Johnson.

3. *Union Leagues* were patriotic and political clubs formed during the Civil War to encourage support for the Union war cause. During Reconstruction, the Union League organized Southern groups which acted as Republican party political agents. These Union Leagues undertook the task of educating freed slaves in politics, and they were particularly important when blacks were enfranchised in the former Confederate states in 1867 and 1868. The Leagues helped freedmen to register and to vote, encouraged them (naturally) to vote Republican, and helped the Republican state parties in the South to win the allegiance of the newly-enfranchised blacks.

    Although there was not necessarily anything improper or illegal about such activities, white Southerners despised and opposed these groups because they were mobilizing blacks and educating them in politics. The Ku Klux Klansmen directed a part of their terror campaign at the Leagues, and their influence declined by 1870 as a result of such disruption.

4. *The term "carpetbaggers"* was used in the South to designate Northerners who had moved to the South during Reconstruction. It was a term of derogation, suggesting that the newcomers were disreputable and unscrupulous vultures who had come to take advantage of the South's prostrate condition. Because the carpetbaggers formed one part of the coalition (with Southern white "scalawags" and freedmen) that supported the Radical Republican state governments in the South, the term also expressed political hostility and bitterness. It is clear that Northerners who went to the South during Reconstruction included a variety of people with a variety of motives. Some fit the stereotype, but many others were schoolteachers, farmers, investors, and businessmen. Some Union soldiers first saw the South during the war, liked what they found, and went back after the war.

5. *The Fourteenth Amendment,* first proposed in 1866 and finally adopted in July 1868, may be the most important amendment to the Constitution after the Bill of Rights. The Fourteenth Amendment made the freed slaves citizens of the United States and of the states in which they lived. This settled the legal status of Negroes who, according to the *Dred Scott* decision (1857), had not been citizens. The amendment then prohibited the states from depriving any citizen of life, liberty, or property without due process of law. This was intended to protect the newly-made citizens from violations of their rights by the Southern state governments. Of course, the amendment also extended this same constitutional protection to all citizens in every state.

   The amendment also reduced the representation of those states that denied the vote to any adult male citizens. The purpose of this was to correct the original constitutional provision that counted three-fifths of the slaves for purposes of representation. Now blacks would count fully for representation only if they were given the right to vote. This section of the Fourteenth Amendment was unenforceable. Next the amendment excluded from officeholding the civil and military leaders of the Confederacy, and it repudiated the Confederate debt.

Map Exercise

Reconstruction

On the map on p. 278 at the back of this Student Guide, using different colors, shade in the following groups of states:

1. Those slave states (or regions) that did not secede from the Union.

2. Those states where Lincoln established provisional Reconstruction governments during the war.

3. Those states where Conservative governments were established prior to the disputed election of 1876.

4. Those states that were still under Republican rule after the disputed election of 1876.

Self-Test

I. Match each identifying statement with the appropriate name.

    a. Fredrick Douglass (532)   c. Thaddeus Stevens (533)
    b. Oliver O. Howard (530)   d. Samuel Tilden (551)

e. Henry Wirtz (527)   g. Henry Cabot Lodge (554)
f. Charles Sumner (538)

1. _____ The Union general who became the first administrator of the Freedmen's Bureau.

2. _____ The Radical Republican congressman who proposed the confiscation of plantations and the parceling of their land out to former slaves.

3. _____ The commander of the Andersonville prison who was the only Confederate executed for war crimes.

4. _____ The Democratic party's presidential nominee who lost the disputed election of 1876 by a single electoral vote.

5. _____ The Radical Republican senator who argued that the Confederate states had committed "state suicide" and could re-enter the Union only under Congressional direction.

II. Match each identifying statement with one of the items below.

a. Thirteenth Amendment (525)   f. Civil Rights Act of 1866
b. Freedmen's Bureau Act (530)   (538)
c. disfranchisement (552)   g. constitutionalism (528)
d. Tenure of Office Act (542)   h. Force Bill (554)
e. Fourteenth Amendment (539)

1. _____ This freed the slaves throughout the United States.

2. _____ With its ratification, the former slaves were, in effect, made citizens of the United States.

3. _____ This seemed to indicate that the national government had quite limited powers to help the former slaves beyond the mere granting of their freedom.

4. _____ This created a postwar refugee agency to help the former slaves adjust to their changed circumstances.

5. _____ President Johnson's violation of this law nearly brought his conviction on impeachment charges in Congress.

III. Circle the phrase that best completes each statement.

1. After the Civil War, most Northerners and Southerners assumed that the rebuilding of the South was the responsibility of   (a) Southerners,   (b) the federal government,   (c) the next generation. (525)

2. Most Northerners assumed after the Civil War that the soundest approach to the economic reconstruction of the South was through the application of   (a) mercantilistic laws,   (b) government aid,   (c) the concept of laissez-faire. (533)

3. Congress's plan for Reconstruction was embodied in the (a) Fourteenth Amendment,   (b) Civil Rights Act of 1866, (c) Wade-Davis Bill. (538)

4. The program of congressional Reconstruction represented   (a) a balance between Moderate and Radical Republicans,   (b) a compromise between the president and Congress,   (c) a compromise between Democrats and Republicans. (541)

5. Most whites in the North and South believed the former slaves were (a) capable of self-government,   (b) inferior to whites, (c) hardworking and thrifty. (545)

6. The Black Codes   (a) were devised by the national government to regulate the former slaves after the war,   (b) for the first time gave blacks an opportunity to participate in political activity, (c) were devised by Southern states to control the former slaves. (546)

7. The Radical state governments in the South under Reconstruction included all of the following *except*   (a) scalawags,   (b) Redeemers,   (c) carpetbaggers. (548, 550)

Answers to the Self-Test

I. 1. b; 2. c; 3. e; 4. d; 5. f
II. 1. a; 2. e; 3. g; 4. b; 5. d
III. 1. a; 2. c; 3. a; 4. a; 5. b; 6. c; 7. b

CHAPTER 21

National Problems, 1865–1877

The Historical Problem

The problem is to understand and explain the influence of postwar nationalism on the North and the West. What were the characteristics and effects of the nationalism generated by the Civil War? How did people in the North and the West respond to efforts to transform their society? How did nationalizing forces conflict with local interests? What were the consequences of these conflicts?

The Historical Problem Answered: The Chapter Thesis

The nationalism generated by the Civil War affected the North and the West as well as the South. The war experience convinced many Northerners that the Union for which so much had been sacrificed embodied the finest aspirations and special destiny of the American people. But American nationalism was tempered by the belief that centralism had to be modified by the preservation of local, autonomous interests and institutions.

This idea permeated American diplomacy, economy, and social relations during the postwar years. American diplomacy was aggressive and expansive, but it was restrained from excessive provocations by the influence of special groups. Population growth and expansion fed a growing economy whose national integration was encouraged by business leadership, transportation improvements, a communications network, and a national currency. Those business groups who were dissatisfied with the nationalizing tendency fought it out over the currency and tariff issues. Widespread political corruption diminished public confidence in the possibilities of politics and revitalized the campaign for civil service reform. Workers and farmers, unhappy with their share of the rewards from an expanding economy, expressed that discontent in a variety of ways and organizations. The farmers were more successful than the workers, largely because the farmers did not threaten the structure of the national economy.

The nationally integrated economy could compromise with special interests on particular issues and would permit local autonomy, but it would not allow anyone to interfere with the capitalistic system.

The Chain of Arguments and Evidence

6. Why did labor protests fail when agricultural protests
   partly succeeded?

People, Places, and Events

1. *Hamilton Fish* (1808-1893) embodied the respectability and prudence of the established classes in his tenure as secretary of state
   under President Grant. Fish was born into the American elite and
   was graduated from Columbia in 1827 before being admitted to the
   New York bar. In politics, Fish was appropriately a Whig and served
   as lieutenant governor (1847-1848) and governor (1849-1850) of
   New York before being elected to the United States Senate (1851-
   1857). He moved into the Republican party when it was organized.
   During the Civil War, he was a Federal commissioner for the relief
   of prisoners.

   As Grant's secretary of state (1869-1877), Hamilton Fish's natural
   caution counteracted the more aggressive inclinations of such foreign-
   policy figures as Senator Charles Sumner, chairman of the Senate
   Foreign Relations Committee. Fish negotiated the Treaty of Washington (1871) which settled the troublesome *Alabama* Claims issue
   with Great Britain resulting from the activities of the Confederate
   raider during the Civil War. In 1875, the secretary of state also negotiated a treaty providing for reciprocal trade relations with Hawaii,
   thus tying the United States closer to those strategic Pacific islands.
   As secretary of state, Hamilton Fish moderated the more adventurous
   tendencies of others and stabilized the administration's somewhat
   disorderly approach to foreign policy.

2. *The Battle of the Little Big Horn* took place on June 25 and 26, 1876,
   on the Little Big Horn River in southeastern Montana. This is the
   most famous Indian battle in American history because it is one of
   the few occasions when the Indians decisively defeated an army unit.
   It also is the stuff of which myths and legends are easily made. The
   Battle of the Little Big Horn happened during the Second Sioux War
   which followed the discovery of gold on the Black Hills reservation.

   George A. Custer (1839-1876) was the cavalry commander during
   this famous incident. A native of Ohio, Custer did not let the fact
   that he graduated last in his West Point class in 1861 prevent him
   from becoming the youngest brigadier general in the Union army
   at the age of twenty-three. During the Civil War, he was popular
   with his troops, admired by the public for his dash and striking appearance (he wore his blonde hair shoulder length), and became an
   able field officer. Remaining in the service at war's end, Custer became

a lieutenant colonel in the Seventh Cavalry in the spasmodic Indian wars in the West.

In the last fateful campaign of the Second Sioux War, Custer was sent to round up hostile Sioux and Cheyenne tribesmen. He unwisely divided his force and unexpectedly ran into an unusually large concentration of Indians while leading only about 260 men. The Indians overwhelmed the outnumbered cavalry force and they were killed to the last man.

3. *William M. ("Boss") Tweed* (1823-1878) is probably the most well-known corruptionist in American history and a symbolic figure in the history of the Gilded Age. Tweed was born in New York City and rose to power in the pyramid of local and state offices, serving as an alderman of New York City, a congressman, state senator, and leader of Tammany Hall (a New York Democratic political club). He laid the foundation for his "ring" during the Civil War.

The Tweed Ring succeeded because it dominated all parts of the government. In New York City, contracts were approved only after the ring was paid from ten to eighty-five percent of the contract total. In 1868, Tweed's man was elected governor, and this opened the state to the depredations of Tweed's gang. In spite of public revelations and cries of rage at such thievery, the Tweed Ring broke only when unhappy members divulged documentary evidence. Tweed was convicted and served a short jail term before fleeing the country to avoid a suit to recover stolen money. He was extradited to the United States and died in jail.

The Tweed Ring is unique because of the scale of its operation (it is estimated that between $30 million and $200 million was stolen from New York), the audacity of the participants, and the difficulty in achieving justice. Only Tweed was punished, although many others were involved.

4. *Rutherford B. Hayes* (1822-1893), who served only one term as president, illustrates the limitations imposed on national leaders by the political balance characteristic of the Gilded Age. Hayes was a native of Ohio who was educated at Kenyon College (1842) and Harvard Law School (1845). He left a legal career and minor political activity as a Whig and then as a Republican to serve in the Union army during the war. He was made a brevet major general which helped his later political career in an age when service in the Union army was a prerequisite for high national office.

He was governor of Ohio for two terms (1868-1872) during which time he won legislative support for the improvement of prison conditions, the revision of railroad regulation, and the creation of Ohio

State University. The Republican party needed Hayes in 1876 to unite the party's factions during the presidential campaign. Hayes did not win a majority of the popular vote, but the electoral commission and the compromise agreements assured his electoral victory.

The irregular circumstances surrounding Hayes's election damaged his ability to lead; he weakened himself further by announcing at the outset that he would serve only one term, an action that deprived him of political leverage. To make matters still worse, the Democrats controlled the House of Representatives for his full term and both houses of Congress during Hayes's last two years.

5. *Munn* v. *Illinois* (1877) was one of a group of cases known collectively as the Granger cases because they tested the so-called Granger Laws by which states regulated railroad and other rate charges. In *Munn* v. *Illinois,* a group of Chicago grain warehousemen challenged an 1873 Illinois law that set the maximum rates for grain storage. The warehousemen argued that the state law was unconstitutional because it infringed on the federal government's constitutional authority to regulate interstate commerce, and because it violated the due process clause of the Fourteenth Amendment.

The Supreme Court voted seven to two to uphold the constitutionality of the Illinois law, holding that it was proper for the state to regulate private property that was used in the public interest, and that such regulation did not violate due process. One of the dissenting opinions, that of Justice Stephen J. Field, argued that it was not sufficient to protect private property rights by following the procedures of due process; the substance of property rights had to be protected as well. This view gained strength later in the century.

6. *"The Crime of '73"* is an event that did not happen, or at least not the way many Americans thought. From 1792 to 1873 United States coinage laws provided that all gold and silver sold to the U.S. mint would be coined. This was called free and unlimited coinage of gold and silver. As it happened, there were few silver dollars minted because the market price of silver made it more profitable to sell silver on the open market rather than to the U.S. mint.

In 1873, the Coinage Act adjusted government policy to its practice by dropping the silver dollar from the list of approved coins. This was called the demonetization of silver, and it made gold the single monetary standard. By chance, at almost the same time, the market price of silver dropped to a point that made it more profitable to sell silver to the U.S. mint at the rates set by Congress. Silver mine owners and those who favored currency inflation saw in the

Coinage Act of 1873 a devious conspiracy by those committed to the gold standard.

7. *The Knights of Labor* was a pioneering labor organization that flourished from 1878 to 1893. The Knights began as a secret group organized by garment workers in Philadelphia in 1869. In 1878 it became a national labor organization. The Knights of Labor was an industrial union that included two types of local organization: trade assemblies organized workers in a single trade or craft; mixed assemblies included all gainfully employed persons, the unskilled as well as farmers and even employers. Only certain professional groups were not eligible for membership. The leader of the Knights from 1879 to 1893 was Terence V. Powderly (1849-1924), and the major growth in membership came between 1878 and 1887 when there were nearly 6,000 local assemblies with a total membership of at least 700,000 Knights.

The Knights of Labor supported the eight-hour day, a graduated income tax, consumers' and producers' cooperatives, boycotts, and arbitration. But they did not accept the strike as a legitimate labor weapon. The antilabor aftermath of the Haymarket Riot in Chicago in 1886 seriously damaged the Knights. By 1893, the organization was dominated by farmers, and Terence Powderly was replaced by an Iowan. This was a strange fate for an innovative labor movement.

Self-Test

I. Match each identifying statement with the appropriate name.

a. Henry George (580)	e. Terence Powderly (580)
b. James Garfield (574)	f. Chester Arthur (573)
c. William Tweed (571)	g. William Seward (558)
d. Oliver H. Kelley (577)	h. Uriah Stephens (580)

1. _____ The President who had little sympathy for civil service reform, but whose assassination by a crazed office seeker led to the passage of the Civil Service Reform (Pendleton) Act in 1883.

2. _____ Author of *Progress and Poverty* who, in 1879, alleged that America's economic troubles resulted from the private ownership of land and the collection of rents.

3. _____ President Johnson's secretary of state who encouraged the French withdrawal from Mexico and who purchased Alaska.

4. _____ The Department of Agriculture clerk who hoped to improve the conditions of American farm life by organizing the Patrons of Husbandry (Grange).

5. _____ Leader of the Knights of Labor during their years of growth who preferred arbitration to strikes as a means of settling labor disputes.

II. Circle the phrase that best completes each statement.

1. During the Civil War, the idea of Union came to mean to many Northerners that (a) the United States would have to be more centralized than it had been in the past, (b) the states were ultimately sovereign, (c) the war had obliterated America's claim to a special destiny. (558)

2. American diplomacy after the Civil War was characterized by (a) popular support for territorial expansion, (b) isolationism, (c) commitment to the balance of power in the Western Hemisphere. (558)

3. The Dawes Severalty Act marked a turning point in Indian policy because it (a) created the first reservations west of the Mississippi, (b) allotted reservation lands to individual Indians, thus anticipating the breakup of the tribes, (c) eliminated reservations and forced the Indians into the mainstream of American life. (564)

4. Most settlers in the West after the Civil War (a) purchased their lands from the federal government, (b) bought land from the railroads, (c) were given their land under the provisions of the Homestead Act. (566-567)

5. The integration of the national economy after the Civil War was encouraged by all of the following *except* (a) the transportation network, (b) government regulations, (c) communications developments. (567)

6. The prevailing view toward tariffs in the Gilded Age was in support of (a) bimetalism, (b) protectionism, (c) resumption. (574)

7. The Granger laws of the early 1870s were passed in support of (a) labor organization, (b) railroad regulation, (c) currency inflation. (579)

Answers to the Self-Test

I. 1. b; 2. a; 3. g; 4. d; 5. e
II. 1. a; 2. a; 3. b; 4. a; 5. b; 6. b; 7. b

PART FIVE

John L. Thomas *Nationalizing the Republic*

1877–1920

Thesis

The Industrial Revolution took place in the fifty years between the Civil War and the First World War. Most Americans found that the benefits of rapid industrialization outweighed the considerable social costs. Growth of both the population and the economy confirmed the idea of progress and reinforced the ideal of unlimited individualism. But the process of economic transformation also prompted calls for control and regulation in order to achieve efficiency and stability. Some businessmen, farmers, and reformers insisted that the American system desperately needed repairs. Although the reformers did not fully agree among themselves, their programs did point toward a new national order that repudiated the permissiveness of Jeffersonianism and updated the nationalism of Alexander Hamilton. The new emphasis on expertise and applied science affected business, law, and politics. During this half century, Americans discovered that the individual lived within a social context.

Chronology

1882   Standard Oil Trust organized

1892   Populist party formed

1896   Republican William McKinley defeats Democrat William Jennings Bryan in presidential election

1898   Spanish-American War

1907   Dillingham Commission investigates "new" immigration

1910   Theodore Roosevelt's "New Nationalism" speech

1912   Woodrow Wilson's "New Freedom" campaign

1913   Armory Show of modern art in New York City

1917   United States enters First World War

1919   U.S. Senate rejects peace treaty and League of Nations

CHAPTER 22

Stabilizing the American Economy

The Historical Problem

The problem is to understand the nature of the economic transformation that took place in America during the late nineteenth century. What conditions affected the nation's economic development? What were the phases of that development? How are the origins and nature of the merger movement to be explained? How did the economic changes affect farmers and industrial workers? What were the consequences of the reorganization of the American economy?

The Historical Problem Answered: The Chapter Thesis

The first phase of America's economic revolution gathered speed after the Civil War and climaxed in the 1890s; it was typified by the organization of the Standard Oil Trust in industry and by the emergence of factory farms in agriculture. The second phase witnessed the growth of industrial and financial mergers beginning in 1898. Business led the merger movement in order to control the considerable instability in the economy. By 1910, monopoly and oligopoly dominated the organization of the American economy. The organization and consolidation of business triggered a reaction in the form of antimonopoly. Opposition to business mergers sprang more from sentiment than from objective evidence of economic damage. Antimonopoly survived as a sentiment, although it was ineffective as a movement.

American farmers faced problems surprisingly similar to those of businessmen, but the traditional idea of agriculture's moral value gave a bitter tone to the political movements that expressed farmers' discontents.

Economic conditions improved after 1900, and farmers learned for themselves the advantages of consolidation and cooperation.

Industrial workers discovered that they, like farmers, did not get a reasonable share of the wealth produced by the modern economy. The workers had considerable difficulty organizing. But with the appearance of the American Federation of Labor, emerged a practical labor leadership who accepted for workers the subordinate role of producers and consumers and who cooperated with management to stabilize the economic system.

The economic transformation of America greatly increased the national wealth but did not eliminate class, regional, and occupational variations in the distribution of that wealth. It seemed to many people that the American dream of abundance had been achieved. Yet the integration of the American economy had also set in motion countercurrents moving toward fragmentation.

The Chain of Arguments and Evidence

a. Had the American dream been changed by the economic revolution?

b. Did the social reality fit the dream?

People, Places, and Events

1. *John D. Rockefeller* (1839-1937) was America's first billionaire, founder of a great American fortune and of a large and active family, and an industrial leader of considerable importance. Rockefeller was born in New York but educated in Cleveland, Ohio, where he went to work as a clerk and bookkeeper before founding a produce company when he was twenty years old.

   Oil was discovered at Titusville, Pennsylvania in 1859, and shortly thereafter Rockefeller went into the oil business with Samuel Andrews who had devised a cheaper method of refining oil. In 1867, Rockefeller organized the Standard Oil Company with himself as president. Three years later, Standard Oil of Ohio refined fourteen percent of all the oil processed in the nation.

   Rockefeller set out to eliminate the chaotic competition in the oil industry, and he succeeded by contriving to have railroads pay Standard Oil rebates, by developing a nationwide distribution system, and by driving out of business competitors who did not sell out to him. His company refined more than ninety percent of America's oil by 1879, and Rockefeller had succeeded in bringing order to the industry by imposing a virtual monopoly on it. In 1882, Rockefeller merged seventy-seven companies into what was known as the Standard Oil Trust. A decision by the Ohio Supreme Court forced this first trust to move its legal home to New Jersey. Standard Oil flourished financially and legally until it was dissolved by a U.S. Supreme Court order in 1911.

   John D. Rockefeller retired about this time, turning over direction of the family enterprises to John D., Jr. The elder Rockefeller devoted a portion of his great fortune to philanthropic endeavors, including the endowment of the University of Chicago in 1892 and the creation of the Rockefeller Foundation in 1913. These activities and the passage of time have helped to convert Rockefeller's public reputation from that of a "robber baron," as many saw him in his lifetime, to that of an industrial statesman and public benefactor.

   The Rockefeller family's wealth and standing today rest on the fortune accumulated by John D., Sr. Several of his grandchildren and great-grandchildren have been active in business and politics. Perhaps the most notable are David (born 1915), former chairman of the

Chase Manhattan Bank, and Nelson (1908-1979), Republican governor of New York (1959-1973) and vice-president of the United States (1974-1976).

2. *J. Pierpont Morgan* (1837-1913) was so completely the archetypical investment banker and capitalist, that his face and figure remain the stereotypical attributes of the plutocrat. J. P. Morgan was born in Connecticut and educated in the United States and Europe. No poor boy who struggled to success, Morgan joined his father's banking firm in London before moving to New York where, a few years later (1860), he founded J. P. Morgan & Company. This firm acted as agent for the senior Morgan's bank, and during the Civil War Morgan dealt in foreign exchange and speculated in gold. Morgan was involved in some other investment banking firms and participated in the reorganization of major eastern railroads. Morgan insisted on having financial control of projects in which he was involved. He was not a banker who provided capital and disassociated himself from the enterprise which the capital was financing.

Because he centralized financial control, the House of Morgan became one of the most powerful financial institutions in the world, and Morgan became one of the most powerful men in the United States. He used his influence to create greater order in the American economy. It was Morgan who bought the Carnegie Steel Company and reorganized it and its major competitors into the United States Steel Company in 1901.

During the financial crisis that followed the panic of 1893, the United States government borrowed $62 million in gold from the House of Morgan to replenish the Treasury's gold reserves. This outraged many agrarian Democrats and others who opposed President Cleveland's financial policy. It suggested to many Americans that Morgan was more powerful than the government of the United States. Later, in the financial panic of 1907, Morgan again helped to stabilize financial conditions. Morgan spent a portion of his considerable wealth on a private art collection that was later given to the Metropolitan Museum of Art.

3. *Samuel Gompers* (1850-1924) was the dominant figure during the formative years of the American Federation of Labor, whose influence has marked the labor movement to the present. Gompers was born in London, the son of a cigarmaker, and he was apprenticed in the same trade. Arriving in New York as a boy of thirteen, Gompers joined the Cigarmakers Union and later became its president. A dedicated unionist, he believed that it was essential for workers to organize in order to deal effectively with their increasingly more powerful and

aggressive employers. He helped to organize the American Federation of Labor in 1886 and was chosen its president, a post he held (with the exception of one year) until his death.

Gompers read but rejected the arguments of socialists, and he developed a completely utilitarian approach to unionism which has been the hallmark of the American Federation of Labor ever since. Gompers believed that the workers should accept the capitalistic system and use collective bargaining to achieve such practical goals as shorter hours, higher pay, and improved working conditions. He believed in unions organized by crafts or skills, a position which virtually abandoned the unskilled labor force. He also rejected the desirability of an independent labor party in politics. During the First World War, Gompers organized the War Committee on Labor that supported the national war effort.

4. *Farmers' Alliances* consisted of the National Farmers' Alliance, or Northern Alliance, whose strength was in the upper Mississippi valley, the Southern Alliance, and the Colored Farmers' National Alliance and Cooperative Union. The Southern Alliance did not accept black members, and so the Colored Farmers' National Alliance was formed to meet the needs of black farmers in the South.

Alliances held social affairs, sponsored such educational activities as lectures on improved farming techniques, and sponsored cooperative buying and selling ventures. Their explorations of agriculture's problems led them to consider such unconventional solutions as government ownership of transportation, communications, and banking systems. During the 1880s, members of the Northern Alliance became involved in a variety of radical agrarian political movements, but Southern Alliance members tended to remain in the Democratic fold.

These Alliances were important in educating farmers about group problems and in raising their level of group self-consciousness. Many Alliance members in the 1890s helped to found the People's party, and others joined or supported the Populist movement.

5. *The Interstate Commerce Commission* was created in 1887 as the first agency of the national government to regulate an area of the economy. The ICC was created when a court decision in 1886 declared that states could not properly regulate interstate railroads. The Interstate Commerce Act forbade discriminatory practices such as rebates and overcharges for short hauls. A five-man commission was created to hear complaints and order changes in railroad policies. But the ICC did not have the power to set rates; the commission had to ask federal courts to issue "cease and desist" orders. Because

of this weakness, the ICC was not at first very effective. In 1906, the Hepburn Act increased the commission to seven members, broadened its authority, and gave it the power to set rates. This considerably strengthened the ICC.

Self-Test

I. Match each identifying statement with the appropriate name.

a. J. Pierpont Morgan (600)
b. William Graham Sumner (597)
c. Henry Bessemer (595)
d. Samuel Gompers (612)
e. John D. Rockefeller (598)

f. William Jennings Bryan (608)
g. Henry Demarest Lloyd (602)
h. Andrew Carnegie (597)

1. _____ The antimonopolist author of *Wealth Against Commonwealth,* written to warn the public against the dangers of concentrations of economic power.

2. _____ The union leader who hoped that organization of craft unions would enable workers to win a fairer share of the wealth produced by industrial capitalism.

3. _____ The investment banker who, by insisting on keeping financial control of the corporate mergers he participated in, made himself a major economic power in America.

4. _____ His "Cross of Gold" speech in 1896 expressed the pent-up rage of farmers who had endured twenty-five years of hard times and public indifference.

5. _____ The English industrial innovator who made the mass production of high grade steel possible and began the modern science of metallurgy.

II. Circle the phrase that best completes each statement.

1. In the late nineteenth century, the national government   (a) closely regulated the national economy,   (b) carefully planned national economic development,   (c) regularly subsidized business activity. (597)

2. The earliest method that business used to limit production and set prices was the   (a) trust,   (b) pool,   (c) regulatory commission. (597)

3. Businessmen considered the movement toward industrial consolidation   (a) a way to increase the amount of competition in com-

merce and manufacturing,   (b) a step toward a more stable and orderly economy,   (c) a step toward socialism. (597)

4. The Sherman Antitrust Act of 1890   (a) outlawed holding companies and trusts,   (b) was used against labor unions more effectively than against trusts,   (c) introduced popular acceptance of government intervention in the economy. (604)

5. In the late nineteenth century, American farmers suffered from (a) declining prices,   (b) low production,   (c) inflated currency. (607)

6. Among other things, the farmers' movements of the late nineteenth century led farmers to achieve   (a) increased involvement in co-operative buying and selling ventures,   (b) firm bonds of cooperation between industrial workers and farmers,   (c) a higher standard of living than city dwellers enjoyed. (609)

7. The economic changes of the last quarter of the nineteenth century produced increases in   (a) labor union membership,   (b) business competition,   (c) national unity. (611, 616)

Answers to the Self-Test

I. 1. g; 2. d; 3. a; 4. f; 5. c
II. 1. c; 2. e; 3. b; 4. b; 5. a; 6. a; 7. a

CHAPTER 23

The Politics of Reform

The Historical Problem

The problem is to understand the function of politics between 1865 and 1890, and to explain the breakup of that political pattern. How was political equilibrium established and maintained during those years? On what did political stability depend? What did politics contribute to the national life? When and why did the politics of stability disintegrate? What political changes began to take place in the 1890s? What new approaches to politics were emerging? How did these changes affect the national parties and the party system?

The Historical Problem Answered: The Chapter Thesis

American politics from the Civil War to the 1890s was a politics of equilibrium that provided the stability notably lacking in the economy. The national parties were run by professional managers who maintained the political equilibrium by using "machines" and by arranging regional balances of power. The two parties were nonideological coalitions of interests, but they differed in real and important ways. The Republican party was pietistic — that is, it expressed a politics of morality and reform. The Democratic party was culturally pluralistic and committed to personal liberty and limited government. Thus the differences between the two national parties were cultural, rather than economic or social.

This orderly political balance began to disintegrate after 1890 as the older politics and politicians came under attack. For example, angry farmers mounted a pietistic countercrusade in the Populist movement.

The national parties exchanged their cultural identities during the presidential campaign of 1896. The Democratic party allied itself with agrarian reformers and Populists under the free silver flag in a pietistic crusade. But the Republicans cast off their pietism and worked out a practical program that appealed to diverse groups, including urban workingmen. The Populist revolt against the traditional political balance and the election of 1896 transformed politics in ways that paralleled the transformation of the economy.

The Chain of Arguments and Evidence

People, Places, and Events

1. *Roscoe Conkling* (1829-1888) was a New York Republican party leader during the Gilded Age. His original political commitment was to the Whig party, but he became a Republican, served in the House of Representatives, and then was a United States senator from New York. Conkling supported the Radical Republican faction during Reconstruction, and he helped to draft the crucial Fourteenth Amendment. Under President Grant, whom he admired and supported without stint, Conkling had sufficient patronage at his disposal to dominate the New York Republican party. In 1880, unhappy with President Hayes who had removed Chester Arthur as customs collector of New York, Conkling tried to talk Grant into running for a third term. In a dispute in 1881 over President Garfield's patronage policies, Conkling resigned from the U.S. Senate, but was not reelected by the New York legislature.

For Conkling, politics was an end in itself, and he was the model machine politician, openly contemptuous of reformers who wanted a civil service merit system. Conkling was also a successful lawyer. In one case before the Supreme Court, he argued that the committee that had drafted the Fourteenth Amendment used the word "person" in the due process clause in order to include corporations under the protection of that amendment. The Court later accepted this argument, and it became a major legal bulwark of corporate rights. Ironically and appropriately, Roscoe Conkling helped to convert the Radical Republicans' vehicle for the protection of freedmen, the Fourteenth Amendment, into a device to protect the power and privileges of corporations.

2. *Henry Clay Frick* (1849-1919) was a businessman and industrialist who served as general manager of Andrew Carnegie's steel company. Frick was a native Pennsylvanian who, at a youthful age, purchased coal lands and made himself a millionaire by the time he was thirty years old. A few years after accomplishing that, Frick began to work with Andrew Carnegie who considered Frick a managerial genius. In 1889, Carnegie sold Frick an interest in the Carnegie Steel Company. As general manager, Frick increased the degree of vertical integration in the company's operations. In 1899, Frick resigned as general manager, but he did play a part in the negotiations for the sale of Carnegie Steel and the merger that created United States Steel. His large art collection was left to the public at his death.

3. *Homestead,* Pennsylvania, was the site of the Homestead Massacre in 1892. A Carnegie Steel Company plant was located at Homestead. When the steel workers struck the plant, Henry Clay Frick, the company general manager, hired strikebreakers and a body of three hundred armed Pinkerton guards to protect the strikebreakers. As the Pinkertons were being towed up the Monongahela River on barges to the plant, striking steel workers fired on them, and a total of ten guards and strikers were killed in the battle that followed. The state militia was called out to ensure that order prevailed and to protect the strikebreakers. The strike was broken, and the union with it. After five months, the workers had to return to their jobs on terms imposed by the company; they had been taught a lesson, according to Frick, "that they will never forget."

   Shortly after the massacre, a Russian anarchist named Alexander Berkman (1870-1936) attempted to assassinate Henry Clay Frick but only wounded him. This incident seemed to confirm popular assumptions about labor agitation being the work of lunatic, radical foreigners, and it turned public opinion against the desperate steel workers. They were not successfully organized into unions until the 1930s.

4. *Jacob Coxey* was an Ohio businessman and Populist whose leadership of Coxey's Army in 1894 demonstrated how completely the national leadership had lost its nerve. As the depression deepened in the winter of 1893-1894, groups of unemployed men in various places formed themselves into so-called "armies." Jacob Coxey of Massillon, Ohio was the "general" of one such group. Coxey suggested that these armies of the jobless should march on Washington to demand that the national government create a work relief program of road building to aid the distressed. Although the call went out to many of these groups of unemployed, only Coxey's Army, about four hundred men, actually reached the capital. There the authorities had Coxey arrested with two other leaders; they were charged with trespassing. Club-wielding police broke up the march, and the national government was saved from these helpless petitioners whose ideas would be put to use in the New Deal period.

5. *Pullman,* Illinois, was the site of the Pullman strike of 1894. Pullman was a company town near Chicago where the Pullman Palace Car Company manufactured Pullman sleeping cars for train travel. When the depression deepened, the Pullman Company laid off some workers and reduced the wages of others in a conventional response to industrial hard times. The company did not reduce the rents that the workers paid in the company houses, and the distress in Pullman was severe. The company would neither arbitrate the workers' grievances nor discuss their problems.

The Pullman workers and Eugene Debs's American Railway Union struck and closed down the railroads in twenty-seven states as union men refused to handle trains with Pullman cars. The attorney general of the United States, former railroad corporation lawyer Richard Olney, saw an opportunity to break the American Railway Union. The government obtained a federal court injunction against interference with the operation of the mails (carried on trains). Ironically, the government injunction was secured under the Sherman Antitrust Act. President Cleveland then dispatched federal troops to end the violence that had broken out and to enforce the injunction. Eugene Debs was jailed; the distress at Pullman continued; and court injunctions became standard devices to prevent strikes and to oppose union activities. Eugene Debs emerged from his imprisonment a convert to socialism.

Self-Test

I. Match each identifying statement with the appropriate name.

a. Jacob Coxey (638)
b. William Jennings Bryan (639)
c. William Tweed (625)
d. Benjamin Harrison (629)

e. Grover Cleveland (629)
f. Mark Hanna (641)
g. William McKinley (641)

1. _____ The presidential nominee of both the Democratic and Populist parties in the 1896 election.

2. _____ Leader of a group of unemployed marchers to Washington, D.C., during the depression of 1893.

3. _____ The boss of New York City government who provided some services and efficiency, but at the cost of political corruption.

4. _____ The president who defined the custodial presidency as independent, comprehensively negative, and not too energetic.

II. Circle the phrase that best completes each statement.

1. Before 1896, the Democratic party was identified with a practical and limited style of politics and government that historians now label as   (a) "pietistic,"   (b) "ritualistic,"   (c) "fusion." (620, 635)

2. National politics during the Gilded Age was characterized by (a) low voter turnouts,   (b) close elections,   (c) weak attachment of voters to either political party. (621, 623)

3. The most reform-minded faction in the Republican party in the Gilded Age was the   (a) Stalwarts,   (b) Half-breeds,   (c) Mugwumps. (626, 628)

4. The only Democrat elected to the presidency during the Gilded Age was   (a) John Garfield,   (b) Grover Cleveland,   (c) Benjamin Harrison. (629)

5. The Pullman strike differed from the Homestead strike in that (a) the Pullman strike was caused by a dispute over wages,   (b) in the Homestead strike, management refused to negotiate with labor representatives,   (c) federal troops were used to end the Pullman strike. (636–637)

6. During his second term, President Cleveland was committed to (a) the gold standard,   (b) high tariff rates,   (c) reducing unemployment. (639)

7. The Republican campaign strategy in 1896 aimed at forming a coalition of (a) urban business and labor, (b) southern and western farmers, (c) free silver and low tariff advocates. (641)

Answers to the Self-Test

I. 1. b; 2. a; 3. c; 4. e
II. 1. b; 2. b; 3. c; 4. b; 5. c; 6. a; 7. a

CHAPTER 24

The Progressive Impulse

The Historical Problem

This chapter explores the nature of progressivism. What explains the emergence of the progressive movement? From what sources did the progressive impulse spring? What were the progressive reform proposals? To what extent was there national unity in the progressive movement? Were the progressives innovators or restorationists? What did they accomplish?

The Historical Problem Answered: The Chapter Thesis

The progressive movement began as a revolt of the middle classes against urban disorder and the incompetence and corruption of the bosses and machines that mismanaged the cities. The progressives came to the conclusion that government at all levels neglected the needs of the people because it was corrupt. Consequently, the progressives called for the replacement of politicians with public experts, bureaucrats who would base government on scientific procedures. Progressives represented the middle class, but did not differ substantially from their opponents or from those who had dominated politics in the years after the Civil War in terms of status, social class, and education.

Progressives varied in their emphases from region to region, and they advanced a considerable variety of reform proposals. The progressives saw the need for greater consolidation, system, and control. Thus the progressives refurbished the Federalist ideal of a managed republic led by men of ability. The muckrakers, one product of the popular magazine press, provided the reformers with an agenda.

On the level of city affairs, the commission and city-manager forms of government were the center of the progressive reform proposals. On the state level, progressives offered new models of political leadership. La Follette's "Wisconsin Idea" depended on an independent regulatory commission directed by experts who had wide administrative latitude. Despite variations from state to state, progressivism measured a shift of power from legislatures to executives supported by administrative agencies. On the national level, Theodore Roosevelt conceived of the presidency in terms similar to those of the Federalists; he believed in the rule of enlightened men. Theodore Roosevelt's presidency established the regulatory principle in the national government and created the beginnings of administrative government in modern America.

The Chain of Arguments and Evidence

People, Places, and Events

1. *Lincoln Steffens* (1866-1936) was perhaps the most original and
   intellectually unconventional of the muckrakers. He was born in
   California and educated at the University of California, from which
   he graduated in 1889. Steffens studied in Europe for three years

before returning to New York where he became a journalist of the type later called muckrakers.

Steffens first devoted his attention to corrupt business practices, exposing businessmen who improperly sought and gained favors from politicians. Steffens was managing editor of *McClure's Magazine* from 1902 to 1906, and he later became associate editor of the *American Magazine* and *Everybody's*. He encouraged other journalists to work on the revelation of municipal corruption as he did. He became a lecturer, but alienated his audience during the 1920s when his radical political ideas offended public tastes. Steffens's support for communist activities did attract a following of intellectuals to him. His later writings, although they gained only a small audience, were provocative because of their criticisms of American culture. His *Autobiography* (1931) is unusually valuable for the view it provides of the intellectual activities and interests of Lincoln Steffens's generation of writers and journalists.

2. *Charles Evans Hughes* (1862-1948) was a progressive governor whose respectability and moderation won him the support and admiration of reformers and conservatives. He later was appointed to the Supreme Court, ran for the presidency, and served as secretary of state; he then was chief justice of the Supreme Court. Hughes was born in New York and educated at Brown University (1881) and Columbia (1884) where he studied law.

He first gained public notice when he acted as counsel for the Stevens Gas Commission which investigated utilities in New York; his name was more widely known after he was counsel for the Armstrong Commission which publicized abuses in the life insurance industry. He was elected governor of New York as a Republican (1906-1910) and earned a reputation as a moderate progressive by, among other reforms, establishing a Public Service Commission. He was appointed an associate justice of the United States Supreme Court after his second term as governor, but he served only from 1910 to 1916 when he resigned to accept the Republican nomination for president. Hughes also was the Progressive party candidate in the 1916 campaign. He ran very well against an incumbent president, but he lost to Wilson when political squabbling between regular Republicans and progressives in California cost Hughes that state and the election. Hughes won 254 electoral votes, and Wilson received 277.

Hughes returned to his law practice until the Republicans again achieved national power with the election of Warren Harding. Harding appointed Hughes secretary of state, and Hughes attempted to achieve what Wilson had failed to accomplish — get the United States to join the League of Nations. The Senate stopped Hughes's plan as it had Wilson's earlier. After his tenure as secretary of state, Hughes returned to private life until 1928 when he sat as a member of the Court of International Justice. In 1930, President Hoover appointed the veteran Hughes chief justice of the Supreme Court. He led the Court during the New Deal period when the Court invalidated decisive New Deal legislation. In 1941, Hughes retired.

3. *Muller* v. *Oregon* was a historic Supreme Court decision handed down in 1908. In 1905, the Court had declared unconstitutional a New York state law setting maximum hours for bakers. In this case, *Lochner* v. *New York,* the Court held that the law in question was an unreasonable interference with the right of employers and employees to contract freely and that the law also was an excessive use of the state's police power. In a famous dissenting opinion in *Lochner* v. *New York,* Justice Holmes criticized the majority view because it was based, he charged, on laissez-faire economic theory.

   In *Muller* v. *Oregon,* the Court found constitutional an Oregon law that set maximum hours for women workers. The Court held that it was a legitimate use of state police power because women were the weaker sex. Among the important aspects of the case was the famous "sociological brief" of Louis Brandeis, who acted as counsel for the state of Oregon. Brandeis put together a mass of medical, economic, and sociological materials to support the need for special legislation to protect women. It was not an argument that some later women's liberation leaders would find convincing, but the fact that the Supreme Court did in 1908 opened new possibilities for protective legislation and for the application of sociological knowledge to law.

4. *The Jungle,* by Upton Sinclair, was published in 1906. Sinclair's novel was bound to be misinterpreted by its middle-class readers who considered it a muckraking exposé of hygienic conditions in the meat packing industry. Sinclair's purpose was, in fact, quite different. Born in Baltimore, Maryland in 1878, he began writing when he was fifteen years old in order to pay for his education. He attended the College of the City of New York and did graduate work at Columbia University. Sinclair's conversion to socialism resulted in *The Jungle*; he wanted the novel to create sympathetic concern for the ghastly working and living conditions of the industrial working classes and to spread the socialist message. He chose the meat packing industry primarily because it offered richer material for some rather obvious symbolism. Whether inevitable or not, readers were more

alarmed by the relatively few pages about filth and disease in meat packing plants than by the many pages about the incredible ordeal of Sinclair's fictional immigrant workers.

The novel made Sinclair famous, earned money, and helped to pass pure food and drug laws. He invested the money in the Helicon Hall Colony, a utopian experiment in New Jersey. Sinclair moved to California in 1915 and ran four times for public office without success. He continued to write, and in 1934 during the Depression, he organized an End Poverty in California league which nearly won the governorship of California for the author of *The Jungle*.

5. *Robert M. La Follette* (1855-1925) was the Wisconsin progressive who achieved national recognition and acclaim but was never able to capture the Republican party's presidential nomination. A native of Wisconsin, La Follette graduated from the University of Wisconsin (1879) and practiced law before being elected to Congress for three terms. Defeated for reelection in 1890 and having broken with the established Republican leadership, he spent ten years building a following in the state. His election to the governorship in 1900 climaxed a long insurgent campaign. His "Wisconsin Idea" made Wisconsin a progressive model for other states and made La Follette the most well-known progressive politician in the nation. The "Wisconsin Idea" became actuality with the passage of a direct primary law, tax reform, the creation of a railroad commission, and the use of technical experts in government.

In 1906, La Follette was elected to the United States Senate where he served three terms. In the Senate, he was the progressive leader and defended a variety of progressive causes. He founded the Progressive Republican League in 1911, but Theodore Roosevelt won the nomination of Republican progressives in 1912 after they had bolted from the Republican convention. In the Senate, La Follette voted against the resolution declaring war on Germany in 1917, opposed United States participation in the League of Nations, and supported investigation of the scandals under Harding's administration. In 1924, "Battling Bob" was the Progressive party candidate for president, but he carried only Wisconsin.

Self-Test

I. Match each identifying statement with the appropriate name.

a. Ida Tarbell (655)   c. Tom Johnson (648)
b. William James (650)   d. Robert La Follette (658)

e. Upton Sinclair (666) g. Lincoln Steffens (648)
f. John Mitchell (665) h. Jane Addams (646)

1. _____ The muckraker whose fictional book *The Jungle* appalled Americans with its description of the practices of the meat packing industry and led to reform legislation.

2. _____ The author of the "Wisconsin Idea" who, while governor of that state, made it a model of progressive reform; he later led the progressive insurgents in the Republican party from his seat in the Senate.

3. _____ Mentor to many young social reformers who advocated an active and pragmatic approach to solving social problems.

4. _____ The canny president of the United Mine Workers who led the anthracite coal miners out on strike in 1902 and forced an arbitrated settlement.

5. _____ The pioneer settlement house worker at Hull House in Chicago whose assessment of urban blight indicted boss politics as corrupt and inefficient.

II. Circle the phrase that best completes each statement.

1. Progressives tended to believe that the ills of modern society could be solved by   (a) technical experts,   (b) limiting the power of government,   (c) renewed attention to the "institutional church." (645)

2. The major influence on the reform ideas of the urban progressives was   (a) the efficiency of the military,   (b) the modern corporation,   (c) Thomas Jefferson's political theory. (652)

3. Muckrakers offered the public   (a) moralistic exposés of public problems,   (b) a systematic analysis of the social structure, (c) somewhat thinly disguised socialist propaganda. (655)

4. In various states, progressives pushed for programs that included all of the following *except*   (a) direct primaries,   (b) regulatory commissions,   (c) government subsidies for small businessmen. (657)

5. By the time he became president, Theodore Roosevelt had come to the conclusion that   (a) free competition was indispensable to American liberties,   (b) the government needed to take action to protect the rights of blacks,   (c) America had to abandon the laissez-faire theory of political economy. (664)

6. Theodore Roosevelt's Square Deal called for   (a) a plan for regulating national economic development,   (b) a program for providing lower tariffs on selected imports,   (c) balancing the power of the presidency and Congress. (664)

7. The Progressives' efforts at political reform led to the increase of (a) voter interest in politics,   (b) presidential power,   (c) competition in business and industry. (669)

Answers to the Self-Test

I. 1. e; 2. d; 3. b; 4. f; 5. h
II. 1. a; 2. b; 3. a; 4. c; 5. c; 6. a; 7. b

CHAPTER 25

Progressives and the Challenge of Pluralism

The Historical Problem

The problem is to understand how and why the diverse conditions of American society affected progressivism. What social and political realities moderated the reform impetus by 1910? What were the sources and nature of Theodore Roosevelt's New Nationalist progressivism? What were those of Woodrow Wilson's New Freedom version of progressivism? What was the social vision expressed in the New Freedom? What was the relationship between these divergent forms of progressivism and the realities of American society?

The Historical Problem Answered: The Chapter Thesis

The pluralistic forces of American society slowed the forward motion of progressive reform. Among national institutions, the Supreme Court was the least sympathetic to the special problems of industrial society. The appointment of Oliver Wendell Holmes, Jr., to the Court strengthened the progressive position because Holmes's legal instrumentalism warned against the judicial imposition of laissez-faire theories.

Political conflict and confusion during President Taft's administration hampered the development of progressivism. Convinced that Taft was unfit to govern, Theodore Roosevelt announced his candidacy in his 1910 New Nationalism speech that converted the Square Deal into a stronger form of nationalism. This form of progressivism created a chasm between progressive and old-guard Republicans, while the 1912 Bull Moose split opened the door to a Democratic victory. The Democrats chose as their progressive candidate Woodrow Wilson, who called for liberation from domination by big business and big government. Influenced by Louis Brandeis, Wilson's New Freedom expressed old-fashioned idealism and moralism.

The influx of large numbers of immigrants from southern and eastern Europe in America prompted progressives to contrive ways to "Americanize" these new arrivals. Some of the younger progressives, however, accepted the ideal of a pluralistic American culture. But progressive anxieties expressed themselves in the Dillingham Commission's distinction between "old" and "new" — that is, less easily assimilable — immigrants. Progressives considered the race problems, on the other hand, to be a peculiarly southern issue, and so they were untroubled by disenfranchisement and segregation.

The women's movement, prompted in part by the number of women in the work force and by the new model offered by the settlement-house women, also ran counter to nationalist-progressive dreams of a more orderly and well-integrated society. The idea of the "New Women" raised perplexing questions about the proper role and status of women in society. Although the women's movement ultimately achieved one objective in the adoption of the Nineteenth Amendment, it did not offer an alternative proposal for reordering American society.

The Socialists did have a distinctive suggestion in their criticisms of capitalism, but socialism in America was so faction-ridden that its main contribution was to provide an example of pluralism in action. Woodrow Wilson's New Freedom recognized the diversities of American life and promised to release them. But in implementing the New Freedom once in office, Wilson's program surrendered to the logic of Roosevelt's New Nationalism. His liberation ideal was beaten, and the reforms he achieved actually strengthened the central government and the bureaucracy. Without intending to do so, Wilson had completed Roosevelt's bureaucratic revolution.

The Chain of Arguments and Evidence

People, Places, and Events

1. *Jane Addams* (1860-1935) was certainly the most influential American
   woman of her generation. Born in Illinois and educated at Rockford
   College (1882), she also attended Women's Medical College in Philadelphia. On a European trip, 1887-1888, she visited some of the
   settlement houses that had been established in city slums by English
   reformers who wanted to bridge the social chasm between classes.
   On her return to the United States, Jane Addams and Ellen Gates
   Starr bought the old Hull mansion in the midst of a Chicago slum and
   began to adapt the settlement-house idea to American circumstances.
   Hull House became an example of practical social reform in action
   for a generation of American women, intellectuals, and reformers.

Her experiences in the slums of Chicago convinced Jane Addams that the traditional middle-class moralistic do-goodism was insufficient to deal with the realities of modern, urban, industrial life. In her writings and public speeches, Jane Addams made herself an eloquent voice on behalf of a new form of social democracy that she hoped would replace the old individualism. Active in politics, she was a progressive innovator in Chicago and in Illinois. At the Progressive party, or Bull Moose, convention in 1912, she seconded the nomination of Theodore Roosevelt. She supported women's suffrage and was an active pacifist, serving as chairman of the Women's Peace party. In 1919, she was corecipient of the Nobel Peace Prize. Among her writings, *Twenty Years at Hull House* (1910) and *Democracy and Social Ethics* (1902) are particularly memorable.

2. *Herbert Croly* (1870-1910) is perhaps the most difficult progressive thinker to classify neatly, although he is usually considered a nationalist. Certainly his *Promise of American Life* (1909) was the most original progressive testament. Croly's family background was not ordinary: his father was an Irish immigrant who became a newspaper editor in New York; his mother was a newspaper journalist and feminist. As a young man, Herbert Croly spent some years in Paris, and Harvard contributed the remainder of his education over an eleven-year period (Croly did not receive a degree from Harvard until 1910). At Harvard, Croly had the good fortune to be influenced by William James, Josiah Royce, and George Santayana.

In *The Promise of American Life,* Croly argued against the Lockean idea that society is composed of individuals who have rights independent of society and government. He also rejected the traditional American assumption that progress was automatic. His book is pervaded by a sense of community, and he found his heroes in Alexander Hamilton, Abraham Lincoln, and Theodore Roosevelt. They understood Croly's call for the government to take responsibility for achieving the "national purpose," which was to him "a morally and socially desirable distribution of wealth."

Croly suggested that large business corporations produced economic benefits, but he did not ignore the corruption and social distress they also caused. He believed that government should be powerful enough to achieve its proper purposes, and so he based his hope for the future on a "new nationalism." Theodore Roosevelt borrowed the phrase to describe his own program in 1912. Croly later became disillusioned with Roosevelt and, after reluctantly supporting Wilson in 1916, he switched to Bob La Follette in 1924. The classic *Promise of American Life* sold only 7,500 copies, but its influence was considerably greater because of the leading men who did read it.

3. *Louis Brandeis* (1856-1941) was a progressive lawyer, shaper of the New Freedom, and Supreme Court justice. Brandeis was born in Louisville, Kentucky, and educated in the public schools, in Germany, and at Harvard Law School (1878). He practiced law in Boston, earning fame as a successful and innovative attorney who used sociological briefs and represented the public interest. His contribution to sociological jurisprudence was especially distinguished in *Muller* v. *Oregon* (see chapter 24).

   Brandeis's advice was sought by Woodrow Wilson, who found Brandeis's opposition to business concentrations and big government congenial. His counsel strengthened Wilson's inclination to pursue policies that would aim at the restoration of competition in business. In 1916, Wilson appointed Brandeis to the Supreme Court, and his confirmation was achieved only after the sturdy opposition of the traditional legal profession had been overcome.

   On the bench, Brandeis joined Oliver Wendell Holmes, Jr., on the side of judicial restraint. He supported a limited role for judicial decision-making while defending the legitimacy of legislative economic regulations. His voice on the Court warned against judicial interference with social and economic experimentation by the states. He retired from the Court in 1939.

4. *Eugene V. Debs* (1855-1926) was the most well-known American socialist leader. Debs was born in Terre Haute, Indiana, where he went to work in the railroad shops at the age of fifteen. He later became a railroad fireman and a member of the Brotherhood of Locomotive Firemen, a craft union. But Debs became a convert to industrial unionism, which aimed at the organization of all the workers in a particular industry rather than by crafts. He was one of the founders and then president of the American Railway Union (1893). As a consequence of the Pullman strike (see chapter 23), Debs and other leaders of the ARU were imprisoned for six months. There Debs studied socialism and concluded that private property had to be abolished. "I am for socialism," he explained later, "because I am for humanity."

   Debs was a "socialist of the heart" rather than an ideologue, and he worked to promote a socialist political movement in the United States. In 1897, he founded the Social Democratic party of America and then in 1900 joined to it a portion of the Socialist Labor party to form the Socialist party of America. He was the party's presidential candidate in five national elections from 1900 to 1920; in 1912 the socialist high point was reached when Debs won six percent of the popular vote.

When the First World War broke out, Debs stuck to the socialist principles and was a pacifist. He was tried under the Espionage Act for sedition and sentenced to ten years in prison because he spoke against the idea of a "patriotic duty." The Supreme Court upheld the sentence, and Debs's 1920 presidential campaign took place while he was in the federal prison in Atlanta; despite that handicap, he managed to get nearly one million votes. When the First World War ended, President Wilson refused to pardon Debs, but Harding did so in 1921.

After his release, Debs found the socialist movement in disarray from the effects of the war and the postwar reaction. He tried without much success to put the pieces back together again. In 1924, Debs acknowledged the pointlessness of the socialist political program by supporting La Follette's Progressive party campaign.

5. *"Wobblies"* was the popular name for the Industrial Workers of the World, one of the most unusual and interesting labor movements in American history. The Wobblies were organized in 1905 as a union for all workers, skilled and unskilled. The Wobblies rejected the craft union approach of the American Federation of Labor, and they had little use for conventional methods of political democracy. They called for "one big union" and urged direct action to abolish the wage system. They worked to organize unskilled and migratory workers in the West, especially in lumbering and fruit growing, but a major success came in a textile strike in Lawrence, Massachusetts, involving mainly immigrant workers. The IWW found it difficult to compete with more conventional unions like the American Federation of Labor, whose accommodation to the capitalistic system appealed to skilled workers in particular.

With the American entry into the First World War, the national government moved to crush the Wobblies even though they hardly represented a danger to the public peace and safety. In some areas, mob violence was used to destroy the "one big union," and the federal government tried and convicted Wobbly leaders like "Big Bill" Haywood. The IWW did not survive the First World War. Its short life was left a lively tradition of radical unionism, the ideal of industrial organization, and some good labor songs.

Map Exercise

Women's Suffrage Before the 19th Amendment

1. On the map on p. 279 at the back of this Student Guide, using different colors, shade in the states that had (a) equal suffrage prior

to passage of the Nineteenth Amendment (b) partial women's suffrage.

2. What does this show you about the way in which the suffrage movement developed?

3. Is it possible to generalize about reform from the suffrage movement?

Self-Test

I. Match each identifying statement with the appropriate name.

a. Gifford Pinchot (677)
b. Florence Kelley (690)
c. Alice Paul (694)
d. William E. B. Du Bois (687)
e. Eugene V. Debs (695)
f. Louis Brandeis (698)
g. "Big Bill" Haywood (696)
h. Booker T. Washington (686)
i. Oliver Wendell Holmes (675)

1. _____ A leader of American blacks who urged the education of a cultural elite as a better way to improve the conditions of black Americans than their dependence on vocational education.

2. _____ Appointed the nation's chief forester by President Roosevelt, he became involved in a party-splitting public controversy with Taft's secretary of the interior, Richard Ballinger.

3. _____ Forceful leader of the Industrial Workers of the World whose reputation for radicalism frightened middle-class America and progressive reformers.

4. _____ Daughter of an abolitionist congressman, she headed the National Consumers' League's lobbying effort for the protection of women and child labor.

5. _____ Leader and oft-times presidential candidate of the Socialist Party of America in the first quarter of the twentieth century.

6. _____ The nation's leading progressive lawyer and the chief architect of Woodrow Wilson's New Freedom program for reform; he was rewarded with an appointment to the Supreme Court in 1916.

II. Circle the best answer.

1. The branch of the national government least responsive to the problems of an industrial society in the early twentieth century was the (a) presidency, (b) Congress, (c) federal judiciary. (675)

2. Theodore Roosevelt's New Nationalism called for   (a) improved regulation of corporations,   (b) completely dismantling the trusts, (c) more effective civil rights laws to protect blacks. (673–674)

3. Progressive goals in Congress were most strongly resisted by the so-called   (a) "Bull Moose" faction,   (b) "insurgents," (c) "Old Guard". (677)

4. American immigration between 1890 and 1910 flowed mainly from (a) southern and eastern Europe,   (b) central Europe, (c) northern and western Europe. (681)

5. The immigrant experience in America included all of the following *except*   (a) government assistance for resettlement and education, (b) working for low wages at unskilled jobs,   (c) the formation of ethnic subcultures in many urban communities. (683)

6. Booker T. Washington's advice to blacks was to have them   (a) improve their manual skills,   (b) demand government aid and protection,   (c) organize a political movement for minority rights. (687)

7. The women's suffrage movement achieved its greatest success when (a) women were allowed to serve in the military services in 1917, (b) the Nineteenth Amendment was adopted in 1920,   (c) the Twentieth Amendment was adopted in 1921. (694)

8. Both Theodore Roosevelt and Woodrow Wilson agreed on the need for   (a) social welfare legislation to aid the helpless,   (b) a strong executive,   (c) more effective antitrust legislation. (698)

Answers to the Self-Test

I. 1. d; 2. a; 3. g; 4. b; 5. e; 6. f
II. 1. c; 2. a; 3. c; 4. a; 5. a; 6. a; 7. b; 8. b

CHAPTER 26

The Path to Power: American Foreign Policy, 1890–1917

The Historical Problem

The problem is to understand the changing role of the United States in international affairs from 1890 to 1917. What was the traditional American foreign policy in the nineteenth century? What new foreign policies did the nation adopt and implement at the end of the nineteenth and beginning of the twentieth centuries? When and why did the United States become involved in international power politics? Why did the United States become involved in the First World War? What did the nation contribute to the war and to the peace settlement?

The Historical Problem Answered: The Chapter Thesis

From the end of the Napoleonic wars to the 1890s, the United States, protected by its geographical isolation, needed no foreign policy other than independence and neutrality. Under such circumstances, American "Manifest Destiny" of continental expansionism flourished.

But as the end of the century neared, several factors pulled the United States into the competitive world of international imperialism. The example of European imperial activities, the desire for foreign markets, and concern about the social crisis at home in the 1890s encouraged Americans to accept the arguments of such theorists as Alfred Thayer Mahan, who urged an expansionist, nationalist policy based on sea power. The insurrection in Cuba ignited public sympathy and helped to rally public opinion behind an interventionist policy. The pressure of imperialism was so great by the end of the Spanish-American War that anti-imperialist objections were swept aside as the United States acquired Guam, Puerto Rico, the Philippines, and Hawaii.

With Theodore Roosevelt's presidency, the leadership of American foreign policy was in the hands of activists who based policy on national interest. Under Roosevelt, national interest meant national egoism, and strife resulted. In the years after the Spanish-American War, Americans learned about the limits of the nation's influence in foreign affairs. The Open Door policy in China, for example, would be effective only if Britain and the United States were determined to enforce it. But when any nation chose to disregard it, the policy was meaningless. The United States' policy in the Caribbean involved the country in constant intervention in the affairs of nations there, intervention that was justified by Roosevelt's corollary to the Monroe Doctrine and exemplified by the acquisition of the Panama Canal Zone. His insistence on executive power tied Roosevelt's foreign policy to his domestic progressivism.

Woodrow Wilson's moral idealism inspired a missionary diplomacy that led directly to intervention and war. Mexico tested Wilson's ideas about moral diplomacy. The results were the United States' occupation of Vera Cruz and little else. The Wilson administration responded to the outbreak of the First World War with a declaration of neutrality that was undermined by two considerations: the United States was not willing to allow the possibility of a German victory; and Wilson did not understand the logic of total war. Relations with Germany steadily deteriorated as Wilson insisted on defending a legalistic and moralistic conception of neutrality rights until war was declared. With this act, the nation had achieved a position of world power, but many Americans were not willing to shoulder the burdens of the empire already achieved and the responsibilities of being a world power.

The Chain of Arguments and Evidence

"The Organized Force of Mankind" — Wilsonian Diplomacy and World War

People, Places, and Events

1. *Alfred Thayer Mahan* (1840-1914) was the theorist of national expansion based on sea power. Mahan was born at West Point, but he attended the Naval Academy at Annapolis and was commissioned a navy officer in 1859 upon his graduation. Mahan became a lecturer in naval history and tactics at the Newport War College in 1866 and also served as president of the War College from 1866 to 1889, and again from 1892 to 1893.

   Mahan's major contribution to strategic theory appeared in 1890 as *The Influence of Sea Power upon History, 1660-1783*; in this work, Mahan argued persuasively that sea power was the decisive factor in the rise and fall of nations and empires. He extended the argument in later books. Mahan's position at the War College and his published writings combined to make him perhaps the most influential naval theorist in modern history. Those Americans attracted to an expansionist foreign policy found in Mahan a scholarly voice supporting their wisdom. Japanese naval officers also read Mahan, whose views reinforced their arguments for increased naval construction. Mahan argued that the United States should increase the size of its merchant fleet, acquire strategically located naval stations, and expand the fighting navy. Mahan retired from the navy in 1896, but his influence continued.

2. *William Randolph Hearst* (1863-1951) was a pioneer of sensationalistic, modern, popular journalism and the formative influence on the development of a major American publishing empire. Hearst was born in San Francisco, son of the owner of the San Francisco *Examiner.* After attending Harvard, he took charge of the *Examiner* and began to experiment with provocative pictures, flashy typography, and news coverage aimed at the cruder instincts of potential readers. Hearst acquired the New York *Morning Journal* in 1895 and launched a wild competition with the other New York papers, including Joseph Pulitzer's *World* which had already explored the possibilities of sensationalism. Hearst and Pulitzer stimulated each other, and the explosion of "yellow journalism" affected public affairs when the papers seized on real and imaginary incidents in Cuba to excite their readers.

   Hearst did not succeed in getting himself elected mayor of New York City, although he tried several times. He did serve two terms in the House of Representatives. His dream of being elected president of the United States was unrealistic. Hearst put together a publishing network that included eighteen newspapers in twelve cities, plus nine magazines and assorted news and photo services. He made himself one of the more spectacular celebrities of California by spending lavishly on an art collection, a castle (San Simeon), and motion pictures.

3. *George Dewey* (1837-1917) was the naval commander who so effectively executed the imperialist policies of the United States in the far Pacific during the Spanish-American War. Dewey was born in Vermont and educated at the Naval Academy from which he was graduated in 1858. During the Civil War, his most important action came when, as executive officer of the *Mississippi*, he participated, under Farragut, in the Battle of New Orleans.

   During the long years after the Civil War, Dewey held a variety of naval posts. In 1897, he was promoted to commodore and given command of the American Asiatic Squadron. Warned that hostilities between Spain and the United States might break out at any time, Dewey held the squadron in a high state of readiness. When he learned that the war had started, he steamed for the Philippines, entered Manila Bay, and destroyed the Spanish fleet in a seven-hour battle. Dewey then kept his squadron in the harbor at Manila when British and German warships arrived later. By remaining, Dewey virtually ensured that the United States would retain the Philippines. Had he immediately sailed away after the Battle of Manila Bay, it is likely that Germany, Britain, or both would have replaced Spanish authority in the islands.

Dewey's brilliant victory (the Americans suffered only eight wounded) made him a national hero; Congress made him an admiral of the navy; and he held the presidency of the General Board of the Navy Department from 1900 to 1917.

4. *The Teller Amendment* was attached to the war resolution adopted by Congress in April 1898. Senator Henry Teller of Colorado proposed the amendment which stated that the United States had no intention of exercising any "sovereignty, jurisdiction, or control" over Cuba once that island had been freed from Spain.

5. *John Hay* (1838-1905) was one of the more versatile men in American public life; he was a poet, novelist, historian, diplomat, and secretary of state. Born in Indiana, Hay graduated from Brown University in Rhode Island, and practiced law in Illinois. Hay and Abraham Lincoln became friends, and when Lincoln became president, Hay served as one of his private secretaries. No public leader has ever had a more able and dedicated secretary. In the 1890s, Hay and Lincoln's other secretary, John G. Nicolay, wrote the first multivolume biography of Lincoln; and they also edited his speeches and other writings.

After the assassination of Lincoln, Hay served a few years at European diplomatic missions. Back in the United States, he worked as a journalist but also published *Pike County Ballads* (1871), *Castilian Days* (1871), and a novel, *The Bread Winners* (1883). After serving as assistant secretary of state and ambassador to Great Britain, Hay was secretary of state under McKinley and Theodore Roosevelt from 1898 to 1905. He issued the famous "Open Door" notes and negotiated the treaties (with Britain, Colombia, and Panama) that ensured American control of the Panama Canal. Hay was also an expansionist who tried to secure the Galapagos Islands and the Virgin Islands.

6. *The Platt Amendment* was attached to the Army Appropriation Bill of 1901 by Senator Orville Platt of Connecticut. Its purpose was to make certain that the United States had the equivalent of a protectorate over Cuba. Most of the provisions of the Platt Amendment were actually written by Secretary of War Elihu Root. They provided that the United States could sell or lease from Cuba land for naval or coaling stations, that the United States could intervene

in Cuba to preserve Cuban independence and maintain law and order, and that Cuba could not enter into a treaty with a foreign power that would impair Cuban independence. The provisions of the amendment were incorporated into the Cuban constitution and then sealed by a treaty in 1903. The treaty was abrogated in 1934. The Platt Amendment undid the idealism of the Teller Amendment and gave the United States a quasi-protectorate over Cuba.

Self-Test

I. Match each identifying statement with the appropriate name.

a. William Howard Taft (720)
b. Elihu Root (719)
c. Alfred Thayer Mahan (706)
d. William Randolph Hearst (708)
e. John Hay (715–716)
f. Grover Cleveland (704)
g. Emilio Aguinaldo (712)
h. Woodrow Wilson (722–723)
i. Dupuy de Lôme (709)

1. _____ Leader of the Filipino insurrection whose resistance to American authority stimulated an anti-imperialist debate in the United States following the war with Spain.

2. _____ Emerged as the most important theorist of American expansion in the late nineteenth century by arguing that sea power was the decisive determinant of American national greatness.

3. _____ Although it had been practiced before, the so-called "dollar diplomacy" which encouraged American capital investment in foreign countries was self-consciously applied during his presidential administration.

4. _____ American troops seized and occupied Vera Cruz and conducted a punitive expedition in northern Mexico as part of his foreign policy.

5. _____ The secretary of state who established America's Open Door policy in China at the beginning of the twentieth century.

6. _____ Publisher of a New York newspaper who excited public sympathy for Cuban revolutionaries when he published several stories describing Spanish atrocities under the reconcentration program.

II. Circle the phrase that best completes each statement.

1. The group least enthusiastic about American possession of the Philippines after the Spanish-American War was   (a) business and banking interests,   (b) most Filipinos,   (c) American church groups. (712)

2. The United States temporarily departed from its tradition of non-intervention in European affairs in the   (a) Algeciras Conference,   (b) Root-Takahira Agreement,   (c) Open Door notes. (716)

3. By World War I, the United States had clearly indicated its intention to have a sphere of influence in   (a) China,   (b) the Middle East,   (c) Latin America. (717)

4. The idea that America had a right and a responsibility to act as a policeman among the nations of the Western Hemisphere was expressed in the   (a) Platt Amendment,   (b) Roosevelt corollary to the Monroe Doctrine,   (c) Teller Amendment. (717–718)

5. The United States actually acquired territory from a Latin American country as a result of a revolutionary uprising in   (a) Mexico,   (b) Colombia,   (c) Venezuela. (718)

6. American progressives generally tended to hope that world peace could be achieved and preserved by   (a) dollar diplomacy,   (b) maintaining the balance of power in Europe,   (c) legal arbitration of international disputes. (721)

7. Prior to the United States' entry into the First World War, the Wilson administration acted on the half-conscious assumption that   (a) the outcome of the war was of no concern to the United States,   (b) the war should be prolonged so that the American economy could derive maximum benefit,   (c) Germany could not be allowed to win the war. (724)

8. As the United States entered the First World War, President Wilson (a) worried that the war experience would lead to intolerance and brutality at home,   (b) was delighted that at last the United States was performing its international duties,   (c) believed that his diplomacy had succeeded. (726)

Answers to the Self-Test

I. 1. g; 2. c; 3. a; 4. h; 5. e; 6. d
II. 1. b; 2. a; 3. c; 4. b; 5. b; 6. c; 7. c; 8. a

CHAPTER 27

Progressivism and the Great War

The Historical Problem

The problem is to understand the impact of the First World War on American society and on progressivism. What military, logistical, and ideological contributions did the United States make to the Allied war cause? How did the war effort affect domestic society? What influence did progressivism have on the war effort? How did the war effort affect progressivism? How did the war experience interact with other changes to influence the cultural life of the nation? How did the war and the peace settlement affect American foreign policy? What role did Wilson play in the peace settlement? Why did the United States refuse to participate in the League of Nations? What was the nation's role in world affairs at the end of the First World War?

The Historical Problem Answered: The Chapter Thesis

The United States provided troops and supplies to the Allies at a decisive point in the war. In order to do so, Americans had to mobilize their society for total war. Some progressives viewed the war as an opportunity to reform administrative and public policy by providing for centralized direction and efficiency. The Wilson administration's efforts to control the wartime economy were not fully successful because the nation simply did not have the bureaucracy necessary to achieve efficiency. In spite of its shortcomings, however, wartime mobilization did complete the alliance between big business and the central government.

When the war ended, businessmen retained their informal connections to government. The nationalist fervor, ignited by participation in the war, perverted progressive civic organizations into patriotic groups that enforced conformity and compelled patriotism. On the national level, the Creel Committee embodied the war-induced impulse toward repression. To a certain extent, the patriotic hysteria of the war was an aberration, but it also sprang from the progressive prescription of autonomous administrative agencies that gave arbitrary power to bureaucratic contrivances.

The war also exposed the cultural conflict between the progressives' moralistic conceptions of art and the seemingly irrational subjectivism of the modernism exhibited in the famous Armory Show. As the Paterson Pageant suggested, artistic modernism seemed to suggest political insurrection. From a different perspective, cultural critics like Van Wyck Brooks and Walter Lippmann analyzed the deficiencies of progressive reform.

Woodrow Wilson applied his progressive ideals to the elaboration of his peace plan that centered on the Fourteen Points and, by the end of the peace conference, the League of Nations. The League, in part, was an international application of the progressive conception of commission government. But Wilson's moral idealism led him to underestimate the extent of the nation's reactionary withdrawal. His refusal to compromise sealed the defeat of the League. With that rejection and the domestic turmoil that enveloped the country in 1919, it was clear that the progressive era had ended.

The Chain of Arguments and Evidence

Slaughter on the Western Front   TEXT PAGES

1. What was the military situation when the United States entered the First World War? — 730–731
2. How did the United States aid the Allied war cause? — 731–732
3. How did American participation influence the ideological aspects of the war? — 732–733

War and the Health of the State

1. How did progressives respond to American involvement in the First World War? — 733–735
   a. What reform possibilities did the war seem to offer? — 734–735
2. What methods did the government use to mobilize the economy for war? — 735–738
   a. What was the administration's labor policy? — 737
3. How successful was wartime planning? — 737–738
   a. How did the war effort influence business? — 737–738
   b. How did the war effort influence labor? — 738
   c. How did the war effort influence the federal bureaucracy? — 738

People, Places, and Events

1. *Bernard Baruch* (1870-1965) became the chairman of the War Industries Board in 1918; he was also a successful Wall Street speculator
   and one of the most well-known public figures in America during his
   mature years. Baruch was graduated from the College of the City of
   New York in 1889 and began a Wall Street career as a stock speculator, eventually becoming a member of the New York Stock Exchange.
      In March of 1918, President Wilson moved Baruch from the advisory
   commission of the Council of National Defense to the chairmanship
   of the War Industries Board. The board had been established by the
   Council of National Defense in order to serve as a coordinating agency
   for war industries and to increase production. To achieve its goals,
   the board was invested with the power to establish priorities, and to
   oversee the manufacture of war materials, price fixing, and the purchase of war supplies for the Allies. Under Baruch's leadership, the
   War Industries Board encouraged the expansion of productive capa-
   cities, standardization of products and processes, and scientific approaches to management. Baruch also attended the peace conference
   as a member of the economic planning staff.
      Baruch appeared again in public life in a similar capacity during the
   Second World War. In 1942, he was named head of a presidential
   fact-finding group appointed to study the critical shortage of rubber,
   and the next year, he became an adviser to the War Mobilization
   Director. At the war's end, President Truman appointed him to the
   United Nations Atomic Energy Commission. In his capacity as United
   States representative to that United Nations commission, Baruch
   proposed that all nuclear materials, knowledge, and facilities be placed
   under international control. This so-called Baruch Plan was not acted

on. Baruch also authored his autobiography and *A Philosophy for Our Times* (1954).

2. *George Creel* (1876-1953) directed the wartime Committee on Public Information that was created in April 1917 by executive order. The committee consisted of the secretary of state, the secretary of war, and the secretary of the navy, and was headed by Creel who was a journalist. The purpose of the committee was to unite public opinion in support of the American war effort. The Creel Committee, as it was called, developed a national publicity campaign using pamphlets, posters, public speakers, motion pictures, news releases, and official statements. The campaign undertaken by Creel's group applied the techniques of modern advertising to the promotion of the war cause. It is one of the few instances in American history of a systematic, nationwide, government propaganda program. Among its consequences was the encouragement of cultural and political conformity.

3. *Greenwich Village* in New York City is one of the most famous places in America. The Village exists as reality and as legend. As reality it consists of the district south of Washington Square in Manhattan, for most of the nineteenth century a quiet residential area amidst the busy city. Washington Square once attracted the American elite. Its quiet and isolation yet proximity to the center of the great city lured Washington Irving, Edgar Allen Poe, Mark Twain, Winslow Homer, and other writers and artists.

At the end of the nineteenth century, the population and income-level of the Village area changed as Italian immigrants replaced native American middle- and upper-class residents. The Italian-Americans made the area seem exotic and colorful, and the changing social composition of the district meant that low rents provided spacious quarters in older houses for artists and writers. Now the Village attracted intellectuals, writers, artists, and the unconventional. Beginning about 1913, the year of the Armory Show, the Village became America's Bohemia, a New World Left Bank refuge for art, intellectual innovation, and unconventional behavior.

The war and its enforced drive for conformity dampened the ardent unconventionality of the Village. The heyday of the Village as America's Bohemia lasted only a short time, from about 1913 to 1917 when reaction and commercialism pushed many artists and writers out of the Village to suburbia. The legend of the Village as Bohemia is so powerful that it suggests a strong natural need in utilitarian America for at least one haven of artistic unconvention.

4. *Henry Cabot Lodge* (1850-1924) was a longtime Republican senator who led the opposition to the Versailles Treaty and American membership in the League of Nations. Lodge began his political career with the advantage of membership in a family (the Cabots) that was well-established in the Massachusetts elite. Lodge served in the Massachusetts legislature before he was elected as a Republican to the House of Representatives, where he served from 1886 to 1893; he then was elected to the United States Senate. He held a Senate seat until his death, rising to the chairmanship of the Senate Foreign Relations Committee and to Senate Majority leader (1918-1924).

Lodge was an ardent nationalist whose ideas on foreign policy generally coincided with those of Theodore Roosevelt. Lodge led the opposition to Wilson's peace treaty and the League during the fight over ratification. The Senate Foreign Relations Committee chaired by Lodge included six irreconcilables, and the committee recommended no fewer than forty-five amendments and four reservations to the treaty. After the reservations were defeated by a combination of moderate Republicans and Democrats, Lodge reported a resolution of ratification with fourteen reservations which did not seriously impair the League, although they did limit American obligations under the League covenant. President Wilson did not agree, however, and he urged the defeat of the resolution; his Democratic supporters joined the irreconcilable Republicans to do just that. Unconditional acceptance of the League and the treaty was defeated by a vote of thirty-eight to fifty-three.

None of Henry Cabot Lodge's children followed their father's political course, but his grandson and namesake (1902-   ) was elected to the Senate in 1939 as a Republican from Massachusetts. The younger Lodge was appointed by President Eisenhower as United States ambassador to the United Nations. He was the unsuccessful vice-presidential candidate on the Republican ticket with Richard Nixon in 1960. Lodge also was United States ambassador to South Vietnam during the American involvement there.

Self-Test

I. Match each identifying statement with the appropriate name.

a. Walter Lippmann (746-747)
b. Henry Cabot Lodge (753)
c. Herbert Hoover (736)
d. Frank P. Walsh (737)
e. George Creel (739)

f. John J. Pershing (732)
g. Bernard Baruch (736)
h. Van Wyck Brooks (746-747)
i. Elizabeth Gurley Flynn (744)

1. _____ Author of *Drift and Mastery* and a critic of progressivism's moralistic aims and aspirations; he accepted World War I as a challenge to America.

2. _____ Administrator of the War Industries Board, which was charged with mobilizing the economy for America's war effort in 1917.

3. _____ Republican chairman of the Senate Foreign Relations Committee who personally disliked President Wilson and led the opposition to the ratification of the Treaty of Versailles and the League of Nations.

4. _____ Head of the Committee on Public Information, the national government's propaganda agency during World War I.

5. _____ Under his direction, the Food Administration was perhaps the most efficient governmental agency during World War I.

6. _____ Commander of American troops in Europe during World War I.

II. Circle the phrase that best completes each statement.

1. Woodrow Wilson conceived of American participation in World War I as (a) a moral crusade for democratic liberalism, (b) a realistic response to an immediate threat to America's national security, (c) a last resort effort to restore the balance of power in Europe. (733)

2. Some of the progressives welcomed the advent of American participation in the First World War because (a) they saw the war as an opportunity to implement some of their ideas about bureaucratic reform, (b) it offered a chance to build a modern army, (c) they hoped that war would lead to the breakup of the industrial combinations of economic power. (735)

3. Perhaps the most important consequence of the national war effort was the (a) damage it inflicted on American agriculture, (b) redistribution of national income it produced, (c) completion of an alliance between big business and government. (736)

4. During the First World War, America's home front was characterized by feverish opposition to (a) nonconformity, (b) the war, (c) the draft. (738-740)

5. The Armory Show stunned many Americans because (a) the realism of the "Ashcan School" was so depressing, (b) the paintings exhibited broke with the tradition of representational and didactic art,

(c) most Americans were unaccustomed to artistic works that expressed moral principles. (743)

6. President Wilson's Fourteen Points called for   (a) war reparations, (b) recognition of national spheres of influence,   (c) freedom of the seas. (748)

7. The Senate refused to ratify the Versailles Treaty primarily because President Wilson   (a) became ill,   (b) refused to compromise, (c) demanded that it be amended. (753)

8. By rejecting the League of Nations in 1919, Americans signaled their unwillingness to embrace the concept of   (a) disarmament, (b) open covenants,   (c) collective security. (754)

Answers to the Self-Test

I. 1. a; 2. g; 3. b; 4. e; 5. c; 6. f
II. 1. a; 2. a; 3. c; 4. a; 5. b; 6. c; 7. b; 8. c

PART SIX

Robert H. Wiebe ## Modernizing the Republic

1920 to the Present

Thesis

At the center of modern American life stands the national political economy whose essential shape had developed by the end of the 1920s. In the aftermath of the First World War, Americans moderated their optimism and idealism, and they began to pursue material satisfactions with more enthusiasm.

Americans' efforts to deal with four primary problems that arose during this period helped shape recent American history and completed the modernization of the Great Republic. The first problem was how to maintain a prosperous economy. America's nationally-integrated economy had taken its essential form by the middle of the 1920s, but the decade ended in depression; and the nation's leaders were unable to find a generally acceptable way to maintain economic stability until the early 1950s. By that time, Democrats and Republicans alike agreed that the national government should use its financial powers to guarantee a healthy economy. The second problem was how to balance authority between national and local politics. A solution appeared to have been found when national politics concerned itself with economic issues while local politics reflected ethnic and cultural concerns. The third problem was the question of the nation's role in world affairs. Here, Americans tried to find a balance between involvement and withdrawal. In the years immediately after the Second World War, national leaders found the menace of communism too threatening to allow peace-time withdrawal, and containment put the United States in the center of international events. The fourth difficulty centered on the values that should guide individuals in a modern society. To this question, there were a variety of conflicting responses.

Finding the answers to these four key problems put new burdens on the central government. During the 1950s and 1960s, national policies threatened to undo the balance between central authority and local autonomy as drives for racial and cultural standards of national behavior clashed with entrenched local interests. In addition, the Vietnam War reduced support for containment. The problem of the individual in modern America compounded these difficulties and produced a revolt against modern American values. Between the mid-1960s and 1980, the four primary problems re-emerged to demand fresh solutions.

Chronology

1920	Ku Klux Klan revitalized
1929	Stock market crash and Great Depression begins
1935	Social Security Act passed; National Labor Relations Act passed
1941	Japan attacks Pearl Harbor; United States enters Second World War
1945	Yalta Conference
1947	Truman Doctrine announced
1950–1953	Korean War
1954	In *Brown v. Board of Education,* Supreme Court outlaws segregation of schools
1964	Gulf of Tonkin Resolution adopted
1969	United States puts first man on the moon
1973	United States withdraws from Vietnam
1974	Richard M. Nixon resigns the presidency
1980	Ronald W. Reagan elected president

CHAPTER 28

The Emergence of the Modern State

The Historical Problem

The problem is to understand the importance of the 1920s in shaping modern American society. What is the nature of the modern American political economy? When did it assume its present structure? How have national and local politics divided their areas of responsibility? What role did the 1920s play in shaping modern American society? What foreign policies did the United States follow during the decade? How did the Great Depression influence the national political economy?

The Historical Problem Answered: The Chapter Thesis

In contrast to popular images of the decade, the 1920s was a period of crucial change and considerable diversity. Although the era opened to scenes of repression and reaction, the later '20s were much more positive in tone and achievement.

During the 1920s, the American political economy assumed its modern structure, as oligopolies and trade associations organized the economy in ways that minimized competition. The central government was expected to assist the national economy, but not to regulate or direct it; the president was given special responsibility for providing assistance to the business community. So prosperous was the economy, that many became convinced that America had entered a "New Era" in which cooperation and capitalism would produce prosperity for all. But at the same time, many Americans lived outside the national economy, and their lives were bounded by local communities whose politics involved cultural and ethnic issues that were kept separate from the primarily economic questions at the center of national politics.

The nation's foreign policy in the '20s revealed a pattern similar to its domestic affairs of the same period. America's foreign policy stressed disengagement from world affairs, but became more moderate by the middle of the decade, when America participated in efforts to stabilize European economic conditions through the Dawes Plan (1924). Although United States policy encouraged economic enterprise overseas, the nation used its power cautiously during these years.

The stock market crash caused a retrenchment that accentuated all the hidden weaknesses of the New Era economy. President Hoover acted on the assumption that the principles of the New Era were sound, and that therefore relatively little needed to be done by the central government. Hoover did adopt countermeasures based on New Era principles, but disaster rather than recovery followed. Hoover's defeat in 1932 indicated that most Americans held the president responsible for the satisfactory operation of the national economy.

The Chain of Arguments and Evidence

People, Places, and Events

1. *Warren G. Harding* (1865-1923) has long been considered the most
   inept of American presidents, but his election and administration are
   very revealing about the state of American society immediately after
   the First World War. Harding was a native of Ohio who attended Ohio
   Central College and briefly studied law before becoming owner and
   editor of the Marion (Ohio) *Star*. Handsome and extremely personable,
   Harding became active in local Republican party activities and was
   elected to the Ohio state senate (1900-1904) and the lieutenant governorship (1904-1906). He was defeated for the Ohio governorship in
   1910, but elected to the United States Senate where he sat from 1915
   to 1921.

   Harding developed a reputation for conventionality and party regularity that made him the choice of Republican party managers when the
   Republican national convention of 1920 deadlocked. Harding's victory
   was a repudiation of Wilsonian idealism and international commitments. Harding's presidency began in an atmosphere of settled calm,
   the "return to normalcy" he had promised, which helped to reduce the
   tensions and bitterness that had accompanied the "Red Scare". It was
   not an insignificant gesture for Harding to pardon Eugene Debs who,
   during the war, had been convicted of violating the sedition provisions
   of the Espionage Act. Harding's domestic policies encouraged the
   expansion of investment and private business by lowering government
   expenditures and taxes on the wealthy; such actions undoubtedly
   contributed to the economic growth and prosperity of the 1920s.

   Unfortunately for him and for the nation, Harding appointed officials in a surprisingly whimsical fashion. Some of those he put in office
   were very capable, but others were incompetent or totally dishonest.
   The latter appointees made Harding's administration synonymous with
   the crudest kind of corruption. Party regularity and amiability did not
   fully prepare him for the presidency. He had just begun to discover the
   scope of the corruption shortly before he died very suddenly while on
   a western trip.

2. *Teapot Dome* is the colorful name of the location in Wyoming of an
   oil reserve that had been set aside with others for the use of the U.S.
   Navy. Teapot Dome loaned its name to one of the more interesting
   cases of public corruption in American history. Teapot Dome and Elk
   Hills (California) had been set aside as oil reserves under the Wilson

and Taft administrations. During Harding's presidency, the secretary of the navy turned control of the reserves over to Secretary of the Interior Albert B. Fall. Fall, in 1922, secretly leased Teapot Dome to a private oil operator named Harry Sinclair, and Elk Hills to another private operator, Edward L. Doheny.

Although these arrangements might have been justified on the grounds that they were advantageous to the government, since nearby private wells were draining the oil reserves, two things happened to make it clear that this was not a normal administrative arrangement. First, Sinclair and Doheny made very large profits from the leases, and Secretary of the Interior Fall accepted money from the two men. In 1921, before the lease was negotiated, Doheny loaned Secretary Fall $100,000 without requiring either interest payments or collateral; after his retirement from the cabinet in 1923, Fall received a $25,000 loan from Sinclair. It was with good reason that a joint congressional resolution charged fraud and corruption, and the government cancelled the oil leases in 1927. Fall was indicted for bribery and conspiracy, convicted of bribery, and sentenced to one year in prison. Sinclair and Doheny were acquitted of bribery charges.

Perhaps the most significant aspect of the Teapot Dome affair is the public reaction to it. Senator Thomas J. Walsh of Montana, who uncovered the corruption, was publicly abused for his efforts. The public and public spokesmen seemed more outraged by the exposures than by the crimes. Nothing would be allowed to blemish the "New Era."

3. *Herbert Hoover* (1874-1964) had the misfortune to climax an enormously successful career in business and government service by serving as president when the Great Depression began. Hoover was an orphan who lived the American dream of self-made success. Born into a Quaker family in Iowa, Hoover was orphaned at the age of seven and then lived with relatives. He worked his way through Stanford and became a mining engineer with worldwide business activities in Australia, China, Africa, Central America, South America, and Russia. He made himself a millionaire as well as an effective administrator.

During the First World War, Hoover became the food administrator in the Wilson administration's war mobilization effort, and used persuasion rather than compulsion to maintain food supplies without rationing. His work as chairman of the Commission for Relief in Belgium and as chairman of the American Relief Committee in London associated his name with philanthropy and relief. It was said at the time that the only individual who emerged from the First World War with his reputation not only intact but enhanced was Herbert Hoover.

The enhancement of his reputation continued during the 1920s when he served as secretary of commerce under Harding and Coolidge and made the Department of Commerce a more energetic and effective supporter of American business consolidation. When Hoover was elected President in 1928, his presidency was expected to be a triumphant crown to a spectacular career. But his earlier successes committed him to policies and approaches that did not work well during the depression; Hoover relied excessively on voluntary cooperation when it should have been clear that businessmen and others could not or would not provide it. Out of office, Hoover warned against the dangers of impenetrable bureaucracy and government with excessive power.

Self-Test

I. Match each identifying statement with the appropriate name.

a. Albert Fall (772)
b. Charles Evans Hughes (777)
c. Andrew Mellon (773)
d. Al Smith (776)

e. George Peek (773)
f. Harry Daugherty (772)
g. Frank B. Kellogg (778)
h. Herbert Hoover (769)

1. _____ Secretary of commerce through most of the 1920s who used governmental leadership to promote business cooperation and self-regulation.

2. _____ The secretary of the interior who became the first cabinet member to serve a prison term because of his involvement in the Teapot Dome scandal.

3. _____ American secretary of state who presided over the disarmament proceedings of the Washington Conference in 1921–1922.

4. _____ American secretary of state who helped author (and involved the United States in) a pact calling for the outlawry of war.

5. _____ A product of New York's Tammany Hall, he became the most controversial politician of the 1920s.

II. Circle the phrase that best completes each statement.

1. The "Red Scare" was a serious threat to   (a) individual civil liberties,   (b) America's war effort in World War I,   (c) American participation in the League of Nations. (764)

2. The National Origins Act of 1924   (a) prescribed a literacy test

for immigrants, (b) restricted immigration in ways that discriminated against southern and eastern Europeans, (c) stopped immigration from Latin America completely. (765)

3. The major purpose of trade associations was to (a) lower prices, (b) exchange production information, (c) reduce competition. (768)

4. Governmental subsidies to agriculture were proposed (a) by the Reconstruction Finance Corporation, (b) at the Washington Conference, (c) in the McNary-Haugen Bill. (773)

5. Probably the most controversial issue of the 1920s was (a) race relations, (b) prohibition, (c) women's suffrage. (774)

6. A major issue of the 1928 presidential campaign was (a) prohibition, (b) the Ku Klux Klan, (c) the World Court. (775)

7. In response to the depression, President Hoover (a) did nothing, (b) closed the banks and the stock market, (c) acted firmly to help businesses help themselves. (782)

Answers to the Self-Test

I. 1. h; 2. a; 3. b; 4. g; 5. d
II. 1. a; 2. b; 3. c; 4. c; 5. b; 6. a; 7. c

CHAPTER 29

The Modern State in Crisis

The Historical Problem

This chapter is concerned with the impact on American society of the New Deal's efforts to solve depression problems and to deal with the collapse of the world order. What did Franklin D. Roosevelt and the New Deal contribute to the modernization of American society? How did Roosevelt and the New Dealers try to resolve the crisis of depression? Why did the New Deal change direction in 1935? How did the New Deal influence the economy and politics? What did the New Deal accomplish? Why did the world order collapse in the late 1930s? Why did the United States become a participant in the Second World War?

The Historical Problem Answered: The Chapter Thesis

Franklin Roosevelt was as firmly committed to the principles of the New Era as Hoover had been, but Roosevelt was much more willing to experiment, and his openness attracted a variety of able advisers and administrators to the New Deal. The first New Deal measures, the National Industrial Recovery Act and the Agricultural Adjustment Act in particular, were based on the practices of the 1920s; they used government power with restraint. But it was clear by late 1934 that the New Deal was not promoting recovery; popular leaders like Huey Long, Charles Coughlin, and Francis Townsend were attracting millions of supporters.

The New Deal then moved in a different direction in 1935 by giving direct government aid to the poor with the WPA, the Social Security Act, and the Wagner Act. To the extent that the New Deal encouraged hope among plain people, it distressed those committed to the traditional socio-economic system. The New Deal programs carefully avoided disturbing the balance between national economic politics and local, cultural politics by allowing localities to implement national programs. The Democratic landslide victory of 1936 meant that the voters had ratified the New Deal policies which gave the central government responsibility for the economy and gave localities responsibility for cultural matters. It was not clear, however, how the national government was to exercise its economic authority. After the New Deal changed direction in 1935, it gradually lost its energy and forward motion. Roosevelt's fight over the Supreme Court damaged his leadership ability, and conflict within the labor movement further weakened the New Deal coalition.

As the New Deal struggled with the consequences of the Great Depression at home, worldwide industrial collapse stimulated economic nationalism. And some countries, notably Japan, Germany, and Italy, undertook imperialistic military adventures that shattered world peace. Traditional American detachment and reliance on investment and trade to implement foreign policy quickly became irrelevant. The outbreak of war in 1939 convinced a growing number of Americans that the United States should support Britain against Nazi Germany. When events forced a choice between involvement and detachment, the nation chose involvement. While the United States provided aid to beleagured Britain, Japan and America drifted into war in the Pacific. Pearl Harbor finally pulled the nation fully into the world conflict.

The Chain of Arguments and Evidence

People, Places, and Events

1. *Harry Hopkins* (1890-1946) became for some during the New Deal the exemplar of the new government liberalism which combined practicality, help for the disadvantaged, and realism. Like Hoover, Harry Hopkins was born in Iowa, but instead of being a mining engineer he became a social worker in New York City in 1912. In 1931 during the depression, Hopkins took over the direction of New York state's relief program under Governor Franklin D. Roosevelt. When Governor Roosevelt became President Roosevelt, Hopkins moved to Washington as federal relief administrator, a post he held from 1933 to 1937.

   Perhaps the distinctive feature of Hopkins's relief work was his inclusive approach and lack of the moralism and sentimentalism often characteristic of more traditional reformers. Under Hopkins, people in every imaginable occupational category, from the unskilled to artists, poets, and playwrights, were put to work. Hopkins's humanitarianism was always practical.

   After serving briefly as secretary of commerce from 1939 to 1940, Hopkins became President Roosevelt's foreign-policy adviser. Hopkins urged American assistance for Britain, and he helped to administer the early Lend-Lease program. His last public service was a mission to Moscow undertaken for President Truman in 1945 to discuss Russian-American differences with Stalin

2. *The National Recovery Administration* (NRA) was created by the National Industrial Recovery Act (NIRA) of 1933, and it embodied the early New Deal's energetic attempts to apply "New Era" principles to the problems of economic collapse. The National Recovery Administration was headed by General Hugh S. Johnson (1882-1942), and it established for each industry a code authority that supposedly represented management, labor, and consumers. In practice, the codes were dominated by businessmen, and labor played only a secondary part, although the NIRA recognized labor's right to organize and bargain collectively.

The National Recovery Administration approved codes of fair competition for industries and trade associations that provided for price fixing, market allocations, production quotas, minimum wages, and maximum hours. The purpose of such agreements, which were exempted from the antitrust laws, was to promote industrial recovery. Using the famous NRA blue eagle flag as an effective symbol, Hugh Johnson led a revivalistic campaign to encourage commitment to the codes by industries and workers. More than five hundred industries adopted codes under the NRA, but there were many criticisms that the NRA encouraged monopolies and domination by a few large firms. In 1935, the Supreme Court held the National Industrial Recovery Act unconstitutional in *Schechter Poultry Corp.* v. *U.S.*

3. *The Atlantic Conference* was held in August 1941 when Winston Churchill and Franklin D. Roosevelt met at Argentia Bay off Newfoundland. Although the United States was still legally neutral, this was in fact the first of the wartime conferences. The meeting produced a joint statement of principle called the Atlantic Charter. The Charter declared that the United States and Britain did not seek any territorial acquisitions, supported self-determination of peoples everywhere, urged cooperative efforts to improve the economic level of people throughout the world, asserted freedom of the seas, called for attainment of freedom of thought, and freedom from want and fear. During the Second World War, other Allies, including the Soviet Union, signed the Atlantic Charter, thus making it a statement of the Allied war principles.

4. *Douglas MacArthur* (1880–1964) was one of the nation's most famous and controversial military leaders. He came by his military career naturally since his father was an army general. After graduating first in his class at West Point in 1903, MacArthur served in a variety of posts, including aide-de-camp to President Theodore Roosevelt. During the First World War, MacArthur saw action in the major campaigns in which Americans participated; he was twice wounded and rose to the command of a division. He served in the Philippines and then as chief of staff of the army from 1930 to 1935. While chief of staff, he implemented President Hoover's order to drive the "Bonus Army" out of Washington in a way that blemished his reputation; MacArthur personally led the units that shoved the unarmed demonstrators from the capital city, and he exhibited too much zeal in what should have been a disagreeable and reluctant task.

He returned to the Philippines where he resigned his commission and accepted the position of field marshal in the Philippine army. But the approach of American entanglement in the Second World

War prompted his recall to active duty in July 1941. When the Japanese attacked the Philippines, MacArthur commanded the defense until it was hopeless; then he escaped to Australia. During the Second World War, he was one of the area commanders in the Pacific theater, leading the Allied drive from Australia through New Guinea to recapture the Philippines. He accepted the formal surrender of the Japanese and then commanded the United States forces that occupied Japan after the war.

When the Korean War broke out in 1950, MacArthur was given command of the United Nations (mainly United States and Korean) forces fighting in South Korea. MacArthur contrived a brilliant military stroke by invading South Korea at Inchon well behind the lines of the North Koreans, but he then overextended his own forces by pushing well into North Korea. MacArthur's military career ended on a sour note when the Chinese intervened to assist the North Koreans in pushing MacArthur's forces back toward the thirty-eighth parallel in a bitter winter campaign in 1950-1951.

MacArthur did not respond well to adversity, and he publicly criticized President Truman's avowed policy of keeping the war a limited one. MacArthur urged that the United States escalate the war by bringing in Nationalist Chinese troops, bombing Manchuria, and blockading China. When the general refused to cease his criticisms of administration policy, President Truman relieved him of command in April 1951. This created national excitement of the first magnitude.

MacArthur returned to the United States where he was acclaimed as a hero in the war against communism and as evidence that the Truman administration was maliciously incompetent. An elaborate congressional investigation allowed the passions of the day to dissipate, and the evidence introduced indicated that the president had good reason to relieve an area commander who tried publicly to undercut the policy of the government. MacArthur was a major hero of conservative Americans, but he did not run for any public office.

Self-Test

I. Match each identifying statement with the appropriate name.

a. Hugh Johnson (789)   f. Huey Long (794-795)
b. Frances Perkins (787)   g. Harry Hopkins (788)
c. Charles Coughlin (795)   h. Cordell Hull (810)
d. Wendell Willkie (808)   i. John L. Lewis (799)
e. Henry Stimson (803)

1. _____ The president of the United Mine Workers who helped found

the Congress of Industrial Organizations (CIO) to organize unskilled workers.

2. _____ The bombastic head of the National Recovery Administration who made the blue eagle nearly synonymous with the New Deal.

3. _____ The popular senator from Louisiana who produced political fright in the Roosevelt administration when his "Share Our Wealth" plan won public support.

4. _____ The director of the Works Progress Administration for Roosevelt's New Deal who later moved from leadership of New Deal relief programs to presidential foreign-policy advisor.

5. _____ Brought to Washington by Roosevelt from his New York administration, she became the first woman to hold a cabinet post.

6. _____ America's secretary of state who, in reacting to Japan's invasion of Manchuria, restated America's commitment to the Open Door and China's territorial integrity in 1932.

II. Circle the phrase that best completes each statement.

1. In response to the depression, President Roosevelt at first (a) did nothing, (b) closed the banks, (c) moved toward socialism. (789)

2. Perhaps the most outstanding aspect of Roosevelt's New Deal was his willingness to (a) spend tax money, (b) "soak the rich," (c) try new approaches to hard problems. (787)

3. The New Deal's original plan for agricultural recovery included all of the following *except* (a) price regulations, (b) export subsidies, (c) acreage controls. (790–791)

4. The most innovative early New Deal measure was the (a) AAA, (b) NIRA, (c) TVA. (792)

5. In 1935, Roosevelt vastly expanded that aspect of the New Deal related to (a) work relief, (b) wage and price controls, (c) aid to failing banks. (795)

6. Roosevelt's conflict with the Supreme Court is important because (a) his attack weakened the prestige of the Court in public opinion, (b) it stopped the leftward drift of the Court's decisions, (c) it damaged Roosevelt's leadership ability. (799)

7. The Roosevelt administration's most important contribution to the

development of the labor movement was   (a) the Fair Labor Standards Act,   (b) the National Labor Relations Act,   (c) Section 7a of the National Industrial Recovery Act. (800)

8. Conservative opposition to Roosevelt and the New Deal developed for all of the following reasons *except*   (a) individuals and interests opposed the expansion of government authority,   (b) some considered the New Deal "socialistic,"   (c) many abandoned their faith in a self-regulating economy. (801)

9. The economic problems of the Great Depression were solved by   (a) the New Deal,   (b) World War II,   (c) the Cold War. (808–809)

10. European nations thought they had effectively stopped Nazi Germany's aggression with the   (a) Nazi-Soviet Pact,   (b) Munich Conference,   (c) Good Neighbor Policy. (804–805)

11. The neutrality laws passed in the late 1930s expressed America's policy on arms sales to European belligerents as   (a) "lend-lease,"   (b) "no sale,"   (c) "cash-and-carry". (806)

Answers to the Self-Test

I. 1. i; 2. a; 3. f, 4. g; 5. b; 6. e
II. 1. b; 2. c; 3. a; 4. c; 5. a; 6. c; 7. b; 8. c; 9. b; 10. b; 11. b

CHAPTER 30

A Global Setting
for the Modern State

The Historical Problem

This chapter examines the relationship between the Second World War and the modernization of American society. How did the war and its aftermath affect American foreign policy, the national economy, and politics? What did the United States contribute to the Allied victory in the war? How did the Allies plan for the postwar years? What caused the Cold War? What was the nation's Cold War policy? How did the Second World War affect the economy? Why was the balance between local and national politics upset? How was a way found to stabilize the national political economy?

The Historical Problem Answered: The Chapter Thesis

The American participation in the Second World War speeded up the modernization of the nation. Events moved the federal government into a managerial position in both domestic and foreign affairs. During the war, the United States directed a global conflict, and these worldwide responsibilities, once assumed, were not abandoned. The American tradition of foreign policy disengagement was ended by the war and its aftermath. And the need to mobilize the domestic economy for war production expanded the central government's role in the national political economy. One crucial issue became finding an acceptable way for the federal government to exercise its new-found power over the economy.

Truman's accession to the presidency changed American policy because Truman did not recognize the legitimacy of a Soviet buffer zone in eastern Europe which Roosevelt seemed to have accepted at Yalta. By the time of the Potsdam Conference in July 1945, Russia and the United States were not able to find a solution to the question of the future of Germany and eastern Europe.

The inheritance of mutual distrust, American assumptions that they should be able to decide the postwar future, Truman's personality, and the influence of State Department advisers all combined to shape American policy expressed in the Truman Doctrine and implemented in the Marshall Plan. The Berlin Blockade seemed to demonstrate the reality of Soviet aggressive intentions. Between March 1947 and April 1949, the United States fundamentally altered its traditional peacetime role in world affairs. The Truman Doctrine offered American assistance to nations everywhere, and the Marshall Plan sustained the economies of western Europe. The Korean War indicated that the United States government interpreted the Truman Doctrine's coverage to include any nation that cooperated with American policies. The war also made clear that containment would be implemented primarily by military power. Such a containment policy won strong public support despite its dramatic departure from the traditions of American foreign policy.

The Second World War did what New Era principles and the New Deal had been unable to accomplish — it brought about economic recovery. Wartime mobilization increased the government's role in the economy, a role that was magnified by the needs of an increasingly fragmented national economy. The splintering of large economic interests into smaller ones meant that a host of special economic interests struggled for government favors. At the same time, an elaborate governmental bureaucracy had developed to deal with the specialized economic interests. The fragmentation of the economy made the central government's economic role all the more crucial, but paradoxically the same fragmentation made it more difficult to find a satisfactory economic policy. National leadership was bound to be ineffective under such circumstances until a policy was found that could meet the needs of the numerous interest-groups and yet keep the central government removed from their affairs.

The fiscal powers of the government — the national budget, the national debt, and monetary policy — provided the mechanisms that made a satisfactory policy possible. President Truman did not feel free to use the fiscal powers in this way, but President Eisenhower was forced to do so by the recession of 1953-1954. His actions made the new national economic policy of using the fiscal powers of the government to maintain the economy bipartisan.

As this happened, the old division between national and local politics broke down under pressure. On the one side, black Americans, losers in the realm of local politics, began to press for the protection of the civil rights of blacks. On another side, domestic anticommunism expressed the fears and frustrations of many locally-oriented Americans. Senator Joseph McCarthy made the local issue of communist subversion a device for achieving remarkable political power. Washington became the focus of racial and cultural issues that had once been firmly committed to the area of local politics, and the old political balance between national and local politics was upset.

The Chain of Arguments and Evidence

People, Places, and Events

1. *Harry S. Truman* (1884–1972) has the distinction of being the president with the most frequently fluctuating public reputation. During his presidency and immediately after he left office, Truman was the object of considerable criticism for his handling of the Korean War and for what some considered to be undignified presidential behavior. In later years, Truman's reputation improved among scholars and

analysts for his foreign-policy decisions and among the public for his reputed ability to make decisions and for his political combativeness. More recently, some scholars have begun to criticize Truman's foreign-policy decisions and his handling of the conversion to a peacetime economy. It is safe to say that Truman's historical reputation will undergo further changes.

Harry Truman was born in Missouri, was educated in the public schools, and worked the family farm near Independence, Missouri from 1906 to 1917. He ventured into the wider world when the First World War took him to Europe as a field artillery officer. After the war, Truman studied law at night and began a political career with the support of Kansas City's political boss, Tom Pendergast. He was a county judge before being elected to the United States Senate from Missouri in 1934 and again in 1940. In the Senate, Truman supported the New Deal and chaired a committee that investigated graft in war contracts.

Roosevelt selected the little-known Truman to be a compromise vice-presidential candidate in 1944. At a time when vice-presidents were largely ignored, Truman had no preparation when Roosevelt died in April 1945. Given the difficulties the new and inexperienced leader faced in 1945 — the war in the Pacific was not yet ended, peace needed to be arranged in Europe, Russia had to be dealt with, complex economic decisions needed to be made to facilitate the transition from war to peace, and Republicans controlled Congress in 1946 — it was unlikely that his decisions would win total public support. A domestic political stalemate meant that there was no possibility of new directions in domestic policics. Consequently, Truman's presidential standing depends and will depend upon evaluations of how well he handled foreign policy during the formative years of the Cold War. Truman's energetic and decisive manner contributed to the strengthening of the executive during the postwar years. His modest, simple, unassuming ways helped to keep the presidency a democratic institution.

2. *Robert A. Taft, Sr.* (1889-1953) was the symbol of Republicanism in the years immediately after the Second World War. Taft was the son of President William Howard Taft, and he inherited his father's conventional Republicanism. Taft was educated at Yale University and Harvard Law School before becoming a lawyer specializing in trust funds. He was elected to the United States Senate from Ohio in 1944, and he served until his death.

Taft's intelligence and conservativism helped to make him a Republican leader in the Senate and the most well-known Republican party

leader in the country before Eisenhower discovered that he was a
Republican. Taft was the most important figure in the Eightieth
Congress, and he gave his name to the Taft-Hartley Act of 1947
which was intended to weaken the power of unions. In general, Taft
opposed the extension of government power in domestic affairs and
the expansion of New Deal programs. In foreign affairs, he was opposed to increasing commitments abroad. He spoke for a return to
what he considered the best of American traditions — freedom for
the individual. If he had been able to have his political way, Senator
Taft would have repealed most of the New Deal legislation. "We
have got to break with the corrupting idea," Taft once said, "that
we can legislate prosperity, legislate equality, legislate opportunity."

Although a wealthy man, Taft's personal life was a model of old-
fashioned simplicity. He wanted very much to be president of the
United States and tried four times to become the Republican presidential candidate. Perhaps it was his distant manner and inability to
be comfortable with crowds of ordinary Americans that prevented
his nomination. Many of his supporters were bitter that Dwight Eisenhower, a political outsider, snatched the Republican nomination from
Taft in 1952. Taft's son, Robert A., Jr. (1917-   ), also sat as a U.S.
Senator from Ohio, but he was defeated in his run for reelection in
1976.

3. *George Marshall* (1880-1959) was the wartime chief of staff who
became President Truman's secretary of state. Marshall was born in
Pennsylvania and educated at Virginia Military Institute from which
he was graduated in 1901. He was commissioned a regular officer
and during the First World War and the 1920s held a variety of staff
posts, including aide to General Pershing from 1919 to 1924. He
served as chief of staff from 1939 to 1945 and was responsible during
that time for overseeing the expansion of the army from about 200,000
men to over 8 million and for the coordination of a vast global war.

After the war, Marshall resigned as chief of staff and undertook a
mission to China for President Truman in a hopeless effort to arrange
some settlement between the Nationalist and communist forces there.
When the communists triumphed in China, Marshall was subjected to
some criticism in the United States, even though there was nothing
either he or the United States could have done to prevent the communist victory there. He served as secretary of state from 1947 to
1949 and as secretary of defense during the Korean War in 1950
and 1951.

Secretary of State Marshall's name is properly honored in the Marshall Plan by which the United States provided about $14 billion dol-

lars through the European Recovery Program to assist western European countries in rebuilding their war-shattered economies. This was a major implementation of the emerging American containment policy, and the Marshall Plan provided indispensable assistance for the postwar development of the European economies. For his part in shaping the European Recovery Program, George Marshall received the Nobel Peace Prize in 1953.

4. *The Truman Doctrine* was announced in President Truman's message to Congress in March 1947. Truman was asking Congress to appropriate $400 million in military and economic aid for Greece and Turkey. The Truman Doctrine, however, did not restrict itself to Greece and Turkey. President Truman argued that there existed in the world a struggle between freedom and totalitarianism. It should be the policy of the United States, he continued, to "help free people to maintain their free institutions and their national integrity against aggressive movements that seek to impose upon them totalitarian regimes. . . ." Many people in America and elsewhere interpreted this as a declaration of ideological warfare against Soviet Russia and communism everywhere in the world. Here was a key statement of what would later be called containment policy. The United States Senate formally endorsed the Truman Doctrine by a vote of 67 to 23, and the House did the same by a vote of 287 to 107.

5. *The "Harlem Renaissance"* flourished in New York City's famous Harlem district after the First World War. The Harlem Renaissance was primarily a literary movement that brought black writers together and encouraged literary and artistic works expressive of the black experience in America. James Weldon Johnson published his *Fifty Years and Other Poems* in 1917, and this work, whose title poem commemorated the fiftieth anniversary of the Emancipation Proclamation, signaled the beginning of the literary movement. Langston Hughes, Countee Cullen, and others contributed poems, novels, and essays. Black musicians drew on folk music and poems by black writers, and they used spirituals, jazz, and "the blues" in their compositions. Two periodicals, *Crisis* and *Opportunity,* were created by the Harlem Renaissance to provide vehicles for the publication of works by black writers and to encourage younger writers. The Harlem Renaissance clearly demonstrated that New York City was the intellectual capital of black Americans, and it raised the cultural self-consciousness of those black Americans whom it touched.

6. *Joseph McCarthy* (1909–1957) is one of the strangest figures in modern American politics. He gave his name to the English language and

remains a controversial person among those who keep the issues of the early 1950s alive. McCarthy was born in Wisconsin, a child of poverty and hard times. He worked his way through law school and began a local political career that was interrupted by military service in the Second World War. After the war, he resumed his political activities and was elected to the U.S. Senate in 1946 as a Republican. McCarthy's early years in the Senate were unremarkable at a time when the nation's Cold War policy was being shaped.

His rise to national fame and political power of a strange sort began in February 1950 when he announced in a speech that he had a list of "card-carrying Communists" who were active officials in the U.S. State Department. This began his remarkable career as an exposer of communists in the government and an accuser of public figures who were "soft on communism." The campaign was remarkable because McCarthy never discovered a single communist in the government, and he developed the technique of making unsubstantiated charges appear to be demonstrations of fact. Because so many of his targets were Democrats or officials in Democratic-led administrations, McCarthy's campaign of innuendo and accusation was given tacit approval by some Republican party leaders. McCarthy was reelected to the Senate in 1952, and it was widely believed that several other Senators owed their defeats to his opposition.

During Eisenhower's administration, McCarthy continued his accusations, and televised hearings convinced many people that he was an unprincipled bully who did not know a communist from a coal-miner. In December 1954, McCarthy was censured by the United States Senate, an action that ended his political prestige and in effect labeled as lies his many accusations. Curiously, his health declined very rapidly after that censure, and he died in 1957. His opponents called McCarthy a liar and a demogogue; his supporters thought that he was a patriot who properly fought communism with its own weapons.

"McCarthyism" may be defined as "a mid-twentieth-century political attitude characterized chiefly by opposition to elements held to be subversive and by the use of tactics involving personal attacks on individuals by means of widely publicized indiscriminate allegations, especially on the basis of unsubstantiated charges."

Self-Test

I. Match each identifying statement with the appropriate name.

a. Henry Wallace (842)   f. George Marshall (830--831)

b. J. Strom Thurmond (843) g. Cordell Hull (825)
c. Dean Acheson (830) h. A. Philip Randolph (848)
d. Joseph McCarthy (851) i. Douglas MacArthur (835)
e. Robert Taft (844-845)

1. _____ When he threatened to organize a protest march on Washington, D. C. in 1941, President Roosevelt signed an executive order prohibiting racial discrimination in hiring in defense industries.

2. _____ A former vice-president, he opposed President Truman's "hard line" against the Soviet Union and was the presidential nominee of the Progressive party in 1948.

3. _____ The principal architect of President Truman's European policy who was primarily responsible for the decision to commit American power to Europe in 1947.

4. _____ Commander of United Nation's troops in the Korean War, he was relieved of that command when he publically opposed President Truman's policy decisions.

5. _____ Roosevelt's secretary of state who deserves a major share of the credit for negotiating the creation of the United Nations.

II. Circle the phrase that best completes each statement.

1. American strategy during the Second World War was to (a) fight a war of attrition, (b) give priority to the European theater of operations against Germany, (c) rely primarily on sea power and America's strategic isolation. (817)

2. America's major contribution to the defeat of Hitler's Germany was (a) its brilliant military leaders, (b) the technique of strategic bombing, (c) its tremendous productivity. (823)

3. During World War II, America's war aim was to (a) reestablish prewar boundaries in Europe and Asia, (b) force the unconditional surrender of both Germany and Japan, (c) destroy European and Asian imperialism. (825)

4. When he became president, Harry S. Truman tried to (a) deny Russia a sphere of influence in eastern Europe, (b) exclude Russia from membership in the United Nations, (c) prevent Russia from declaring war on Japan. (828)

5. State Department officials who influenced Truman's foreign policy toward Russia after 1945 argued for a policy of   (a) accommodation,   (b) isolationism,   (c) containment. (831, 836)

6. President Truman sought justification for the postwar period made in Korea in the   (a) North Atlantic Alliance,   (b) United Nations Charter,   (c) Marshall Plan. (835)

7. The national government dealt with the economic problems of World War II by   (a) reducing income taxes,   (b) lowering the cost of living,   (c) limiting wage and price increases. (838)

8. The only major domestic preparation for the postwar period made by the United States from 1941 to 1945 was   (a) the passage of the GI Bill,   (b) the decision to continue the Office of Price Administration into the postwar period,   (c) the formation of an economic planning office within the executive branch of the national government. (840)

9. President Eisenhower's major contribution to domestic policy was his   (a) return to laissez-faire economic practices,   (b) extension of New Deal welfare measures,   (c) endorsement of the use of the fiscal powers of the government to manage the economy. (845)

10. The national movement for black rights during the 1940s received most of its support from   (a) the National Association for the Advancement of Colored People,   (b) President Roosevelt,   (c) Congress. (847)

11. The balance between national and local politics was upset by   (a) the recession of 1953-1954,   (b) anticommunism,   (c) the Democratic party. (850)

Answers to the Self-Test

I. 1. h; 2. a; 3. c; 4. i; 5. g

II. 1. b; 2. c; 3. b; 4. a; 5. c; 6. b; 7. c; 8. a; 9. c; 10. a; 11. b

CHAPTER 31

Modern Culture

The Historical Problem

The problem is to understand and explain the development of American cultural values and aspirations in the modern period. What is modern consumerism? How did national consumerism affect the lives and values of Americans? To what extent did traditional values and modern values come into conflict? What problems did modern society pose for the individual? What solutions did intellectuals, critics, and the mass media offer the individual in modern culture?

The Historical Problem Answered: The Chapter Thesis

At the center of the modernization of everyday American life was the phenomenon of mass consumerism that offered increasingly standardized goods and experiences as well as a new model of the good life. The new way of life stressed occupational success and tended to separate career from private life, thus reducing the constraints imposed on behavior by traditional rules. Leisure assumed more importance, and the area of private choice (in consumption of alcoholic beverages, for example) expanded. Changing values made the family less decisive in the determination of status, freed women from the major share of the responsibility for preserving morals, and changed child-rearing practices which were now more geared to success in the occupational world.

These developments encouraged both cultural unity and divisiveness. They unified those Americans who shared the newer values by providing common, national standards, but these same changes stimulated greater awareness of the cultural differences and distances between various groups of Americans. Many Americans continued to live their lives according to traditional values, and they found institutional support in the evangelical Protestant denominations or in Roman Catholicism. But opposition to modern values usually involved some kind of compromise between traditional and modern ways of behaving.

Writers and social critics explored the problem of the individual in modern society. In the 1920s, F. Scott Fitzgerald and Ernest Hemingway called for greater detachment on the part of individuals. The popular mass media offered individuals compensatory fantasies.

During the years after the Second World War, four answers to the problem of the individual were suggested. One said that the individual had to learn the skills required by the modern occupational system and apply them in order to succeed. The second urged individuals to find a basis for values outside modern science — in humanism, for example. A third group, Ayn Rand and Mickey Spillane for two, insisted that the individual was still sovereign. The fourth answer predicted the destruction of the individual. The literary figure of "the Southern" was a distinctively American depiction of the doomed individual. By the mid-twentieth century, Americans were committed to mass consumerism and worried about the future of the individual. Traditional values and modern ones were combined in a number of different ways.

The Chain of Arguments and Evidence

People, Places, and Events

1. *Margaret Sanger* (1883-1966), a pioneer advocate of birth control and family planning, was for a time the most despised woman in America. One of eleven children, she became a public-health nurse in New York City.

   Margaret Sanger's work as a public-health nurse among the city's poor convinced her that excessive childbearing adversely affected poor women. As a result, she began her campaign to make information available on contraception practices and devices. She publicly advocated birth control (a phrase she also coined). As a part of her campaign, she published *Women Rebel* for which she was indicted on a charge of publishing obscene material after the post office had seized it. In 1916, Margaret Sanger and her sister set up the first birth-control clinic. For this, they were convicted of violating a law prohibiting dissemination of birth-control information, and they were sentenced to a month in prison. Margaret Sanger argued that every woman had a right to what she called "voluntary motherhood," and that birth control would help emancipate women.

   In 1921, the first birth-control conference in America was held, and Margaret Sanger's campaign culminated in 1937 when the courts allowed physicians to provide birth-control information. She published *Women and the New Race* (1920), *My Fight for Birth Control* (1931), and *Margaret Sanger: An Autobiography* (1938). Margaret Sanger should properly be included as a forerunner of the modern movement for women's liberation.

2. *Henry Ford, Sr.,* (1863-1947) was a pioneer automobile manufacturer and popular American hero of the 1920s. He was born in Michigan where he had some formal schooling before going to work at

the age of sixteen as an apprentice and repairman for a farm machinery company. Ford ran a sawmill for a time and then went to work for the Edison Illuminating Company in Detroit. On his own, he labored on the development of the internal combustion engine as a power plant for a vehicle. By 1896, he had developed and built his first automobile.

He organized the Ford Motor Company in 1903, which used assembly-line techniques to turn out a relatively inexpensive Model T (popularly known as the "flivver" or Tin Lizzie). Ford's use of standardized production techniques and the assembly line made him an industrial pioneer and a wealthy man. In 1914, he set a standard eight-hour day and $5 minimum wage for his workers, both of which were unusually liberal for the day, and he also instituted profit-sharing. Although Ford was enlightened in many ways about treatment of his workers, he was also very paternalistic, preferring to grant benefits to them rather than have them organize unions to assert their own rights. He was president of Ford Motor Company from 1903 to 1919 and again from 1943 to 1945 when his grandson Henry Ford II took over the presidency.

In his lifetime, Ford was widely admired as a mechanical genius and as an example of the success ideal; he was the archetypical poor boy who worked hard and became an enormous industrial success. In his later years the man who freed so many Americans from locality and tradition by providing inexpensive automobiles paradoxically spent part of his fortune collecting the artifacts of America's rural, agricultural past. The museum at Dearborn celebrated the arcadian America Henry Ford helped to destroy. He also spent a portion of his vast fortune disseminating anti-Semitic literature in one of the few sustained American efforts to spread anti-Semitic ideas. During the 1930s, Henry Ford's reputation was damaged by his refusal to cooperate with the National Recovery Administration.

3. *Reinhold Niebuhr* (1892–1971) is the most important American theologian of the twentieth century. Niebuhr was born in Missouri and educated at Elmhurst College, Eden Theological Seminary, and Yale Divinity School. Ordained in the Evangelical Synod of North America, he first served a parish in the industrial slums of Detroit from 1915 to 1928. He was profoundly influenced by the First World War and by the experience of life in a modern industrial society. In 1928, Niebuhr joined the faculty of Union Theological Seminary in New York where he taught and wrote until his retirement in 1960.

The First World War and the industrial realities of Detroit changed Niebuhr's theological thinking in a number of ways. In general, they stripped from him the moralistic optimism of the Social Gospel tradition with which he had begun his pastoral career. He abandoned the idea that progress was inevitable and that moral actions were easily distinguishable into good and evil.

Niebuhr became the leading architect of what came to be called Protestant neo-orthodoxy, which reemphasized a reformulation of the doctrine of original sin and stressed the human frailties in all moral judgments. His *Moral Man and Immoral Society* (1932) criticized the traditional Protestant tendency to apply the ethical principles that are appropriate to individuals to societies and nations. Among other things, he argued that it was virtually impossible to achieve just relations between nations, classes, and races. Here was a dramatic departure from the usual optimism about social issues found in American Social Gospel Protestantism. His *The Nature and Destiny of Man* (2 vols., 1941–1943) stated his fundamental theology, and *The Irony of American History* (1952) applied his critical mind to the historical development of the American people.

Niebuhr's neo-orthodoxy was attractive to many Americans who did not share Niebuhr's religious ideas. His religious thought defended the proposition that many of the problems of modern man and modern society are not solvable. This was a notion that was increasingly plausible to many Americans.

4. *Yoknapatawpha County* existed in the imagination of William Faulkner (1897–1962) and lives on in his fiction. The county is located in northern Mississippi, and Jefferson is the county seat, but it can be found only in Faulkner's prose and not on a road map. Faulkner wrote about Mississippi naturally since he was born and educated there, attending the University of Mississippi from 1919 to 1921. He later made Oxford, Mississippi his home, and there he wrote his numerous short stories and novels about the Compsons, Sartorises, Snopeses, McCaslins, and other inhabitants of Yoknapatawpha County.

The atmosphere of Faulkner's South is heavy with the odors of decline, decay, repressed madness, and degeneration. His fiction traces the development of the South from frontier days to the advent of the New South of commercialism and industrialism. Faulkner's complex prose style disturbs some readers and critics, but he certainly is one of the most inventive American writers of this century. His Yoknapatawpha County epitomizes the literary treatment of the American South as a land of anguish and decay. Among his many publications are *Sartoris* (1929), *The Sound and the Fury* (1929), *Light in August* (1932), *The Hamlet* (1940), and *Intruder in the*

Dust (1948). Faulkner was awarded the Nobel Prize for literature in 1950.

Self-Test

I. Match each identifying statement with the appropriate name.

a. Henry Ford (865)   f. Ernest Hemingway (867)
b. Ayn Rand (875)   g. Mike Hammer (875)
c. Charles Lindbergh (869)   h. William Faulkner (876)
d. Arthur Miller (873)   i. Margaret Sanger (859–860)
e. Reinhold Niebuhr (874)

1. _____ Her novel, *The Fountainhead,* asserted the right of the creative individual to disobey society's conventional rules in order to fulfill his own genius.

2. _____ In his *A Farewell to Arms,* he developed the theme that the individual could best protect himself by maintaining an intellectual detachment from events.

3. _____ The greatest American hero of the 1920s, he seemed to embody individual courage, resourcefulness, and modesty.

4. _____ Began and effectively led the movement to make birth-control information available to American women in the 1920s.

5. _____ One of the literary creators of "the Southern" whose characters talked more than they acted while seeming to suffocate in a decaying atmosphere.

6. _____ The leading theological "realist" who argued that Americans would have to learn to accept the limits of human possibilities.

II. Circle the phrase that best completes each statement.

1. A major effect of modern consumerism was that it increased the level of   (a) literacy,   (b) specialization,   (c) social order. (858)

2. During the 1920s, sex   (a) became available for rational discussion, (b) was commercialized into a multimillion-dollar pornography business,   (c) became a part of most public school curriculums. (859)

3. The emerging importance of the consumer caused local economies to be unusually influenced by the preferences of   (a) blacks, (b) women,   (c) small business. (861)

4. In the 1920s, successful Americans adopted and applied to society the

psychological principles of   (a) interpersonal relations,   (b) psychoanalysis,   (c) behaviorism. (862)

5. The main source of resistance to the spread of modern values in the 1920s was the   (a) professions,   (b) public schools, (c) churches. (863)

6. In the 1920s, Henry Ford was greatly admired for his   (a) business success,   (b) public service,   (c) personal charm. (865)

Answers to the Self-Test

I. 1. b; 2. f; 3. c; 4. i; 5. h; 6. e
II. 1. b; 2. a; 3. b; 4. c; 5. c; 6. a

CHAPTER 32

The Consequences of Modernization

The Historical Problem

The problem is to understand how modernization influenced American politics, culture, and foreign policy. How did modernization nationalize American culture? Why did nationalization produce conflict rather than unity? How did containment policy work? How did nationalization of culture affect the problem of the individual? What produced a social crisis in the 1960s?

The Historical Problem Answered: The Chapter Thesis

The process of modernization also nationalized politics, foreign policy, and American values. In the 1950s, it seemed that the future of the society was firmly under control as mass consumerism expanded, and the public placed its trust in the value of expertise and in the central government's capacity to maintain a healthy economy. There was little opposition to or disagreement with the foreign policy of containment, which relied primarily on military power to resist communist expansion. The military budget now dominated national peacetime expenditures, but the military-industrial complex was too decentralized to act as a single interest. Multinational corporations also connected the domestic economy to the international economy as American business expanded after the Second World War. Presidents Eisenhower and Kennedy maintained the continuity of American foreign policy, which was committed to the support of international stability. Increasingly, Cold War leaders on both sides acted cautiously and transformed the volatile Cold War to a less dangerous Cold Peace.

The modernization of society made the office of the president responsible for both the health of the economy and foreign relations. The presidency became detached from the normal pattern of party electoral politics, and new requirements for effective national leadership appeared. Eisenhower first met the demands on the modern presidency.

Serious conflicts began to appear when the power of the central government intruded into the area of local race relations after the 1954 school desegregation decision. Martin Luther King, Jr., and President Lyndon Johnson provided different kinds of leadership for the civil rights movement. Johnson's legislative accomplishments in the Civil Rights Bills of 1964 and 1965 climaxed one phase of the civil rights movement. But many whites continued to resist the civil rights movement, especially because they perceived it as part of a larger movement to eliminate local cultural autonomy. In this way, the process of nationalization generated social conflict rather than consensus.

A second crisis developed as the disparity between containment policy and the diversity of the world became evident. The basic assumptions about the unity of communism disintegrated when confronted by the actual diversity of Asian and African nationalisms. The Vietnam War accelerated the disintegration of these Cold War beliefs.

A third crisis developed when nationalization appeared to decrease the importance of the individual in the modern world. Some people began to look outside of their work for satisfaction, and more people became interested in such expressions of personal power as strong presidents and power sports. The youth rebellion also dealt with the problem of the individual, as it criticized the values of successful Americans. But the youth movement alienated many adults, as it became more extreme. The most lasting result of the rebellious 1960s was the women's liberation movement.

Early in 1968, it seemed as if the force of reform and protest might secure control of the national government. But reactions to ghetto violence, racial integration, and judicial restraints on police power produced a counterattack that submerged the election campaign of 1968 in bitterness and anger. Nationalization had divided the American people.

The Chain of Arguments and Evidence

Unity and Progress	TEXT PAGES
1. In what sense were the 1950s years of fulfillment?	880-881
2. What were the sources of Americans' sense of confidence in the 1950s?	881
a. What was the nature of resurgent consumerism?	881
(1) What were the cultural consequences of consumerism?	881-882

Counterattack

People, Places, and Events

1. *Dwight D. Eisenhower* (1890-1969) was a soldier who became the most popular American president in the period after the Second World War. Eisenhower was born in Texas but grew up in Kansas. He was graduated from West Point in 1915, held a variety of commands, and attended a number of command and staff schools during and after the First World War. Under General Douglas MacArthur, Eisenhower was assistant military adviser to the Philippine Commonwealth from 1935 to 1939. Lieutenant Colonel Eisenhower was named chief of the War Plans Division of the Office of Chief of Staff in 1939. Eisenhower was one of the most experienced officers in the army, although not the most senior, when he was given command of American forces in the European Theater in June 1942. He directed the Allied invasion of North Africa in November 1942, and he took command of the Allied forces in western Europe in January 1944. Eisenhower's leadership of the successful campaign against Germany was notable for his skill in handling difficult subordinates rather than for his strategic daring.

   After the war, he commanded the United States occupation zone in Germany and became chief of staff. Resigning from the army, Eisenhower was made president of Columbia University, but left that post to become the first supreme commander of North Atlantic Treaty Organization armed forces.

   Although he had had no domestic political experience at all, Eisenhower's sterling reputation as a great war leader made him a natural for elective office, and representatives of both parties tried to interest him in running. In 1952, Eisenhower decided to seek the Republican presidential nomination which he won from Senator Robert Taft. Eisenhower quickly warmed to the political campaign trail, and he succeeded in projecting his personality to the American people. Although not everyone agrees on the quality of his performance as president, it is clear that Eisenhower might have been one of the great politicians of the century if he had begun his career sooner. He learned the political arts very quickly and was especially effective in projecting an image of honesty, rectitude, and dignity.

2. *John Foster Dulles* (1888-1959) served as secretary of state under President Eisenhower from 1953 to 1959. Dulles was educated at Princeton University, Paris, Sorbonne, and George Washington University. Trained as a lawyer, he was involved in both law and diplomacy early in his public career. He was legal counsel to the American peace commissioners at the end of the First World War, and he represented the United States at the 1933 war reparations conference held in Berlin. His law practice involved large international business firms whose interests he represented.

   In 1945, Dulles was foreign-policy adviser to Republican Senator Arthur Vandenberg and was appointed a delegate to the United Nations General Assembly in 1946, 1947, and 1950. Dulles emerged as a leading articulator of foreign-policy positions among Republicans, and he drafted the foreign-policy portions of the 1952 Republican party platform. As Eisenhower's secretary of state, he spoke out vigorously and aggressively against the evils and dangers of communism. His public statements seemed to suggest that United States policy should be to reduce the areas under communist domination. But his actual policies were more consistent with containment than with Dulles's more militant rhetoric. As secretary of state, he helped to set the modern pattern of the office by traveling extensively throughout the world.

3. *Barry Goldwater* (1909–) is a Republican party leader and United States Senator from Arizona. Goldwater is a native of Phoenix, Arizona, where his family owns a department store which he joined in 1929. During the Second World War, Goldwater served in the army air force from 1941 to 1945, and in the postwar years he remained in the air force reserve, rising to the rank of general.

   In 1950, he entered politics and was elected to the United States Senate in 1953. In the Senate, Goldwater made himself a spokesman for conservatism and became by 1964 the leading Republican party conservative. Goldwater's *Conscience of a Conservative* (1960) and other popular writings urged that the United States' objective in the Cold War should be to achieve "victory" over communism. He called for a powerful military defense and the reduction of virtually every other activity of the central government. His admirers saw in Goldwater an honest, unpolished, old-fashioned prophet calling for a return to a simpler and better America. His critics suggested that Goldwater oversimplified complex problems, and that his laissez-faire economics had been found wanting in the late nineteenth century.

Goldwater was a popular speaker and an effective fund-raiser for the Republican party, and in 1964 his dedication to the party and his hard work won him the presidential nomination. Campaigning against incumbent President Lyndon Johnson, Goldwater sometimes acted as if he would rather make moral points than win votes. Many voters perceived him as a man who would radically disassemble the welfare provisions that had been established under the New Deal. The overwhelming victory by Johnson suggested that most Americans did not want to repudiate the New Deal.

4. *Martin Luther King, Jr.,* (1929-1968) was the most important leader of the civil rights movement in the 1950s and 1960s. He was born in Georgia, the son of a minister, and educated at Morehouse College, Crozer Theological Seminary, and Boston University. He was a minister in Montgomery, Alabama when a black protest against racial segregation on the city's buses began spontaneously. King took the lead in organizing an effective black boycott of the city's buses that lasted for just over a year in 1955 and 1956.

The boycott and King's eloquence and dignity attracted national attention to the civil rights movement, and King became the national leader of the moderate civil rights movement. He directed the Southern Christian Leadership Conference which was committed to nonviolent, direct-action protests against segregation. The SCLC made particularly effective use of sit-ins and peaceful public demonstrations. When supporters of segregation met these peaceful demonstrations with violence — police dogs, cattle prods, club-wielding policemen, and mass arrests — national publicity put majority public opinion in the rest of the country firmly on the side of King and the moderate civil rights movement.

Many people considered Martin Luther King, Jr., a dangerous radical, and the Federal Bureau of Investigation carried on a secret campaign to harass and discredit him. King was frequently arrested for violating state segregation laws, and his writings are among the more effective modern defenses of the right of civil disobedience. The civil rights movement and public opinion were the forces that made the passage of the major civil rights acts of the Johnson administration possible.

In 1968 when King was in Memphis, Tennessee to support a strike by black garbage men, he was murdered. The assassination of Martin Luther King, Jr., sparked violent expressions of rage and frustration in black communities across the country. The civil rights movement had lost its most able and effective leader.

5. *Civil Rights Acts* of 1964 and 1965 were the major contributions of Lyndon Johnson's administration to the cause of social justice in America. The 1964 act prohibited racial discrimination in voting laws, in the use of federal funds, and in such public facilities as restaurants and hotels. To eliminate racial and sex discrimination in employment, the act established the Equal Employment Opportunities Commission. The Voting Rights Act of 1965 was designed to enforce the provisions of the Fifteenth Amendment by protecting black voting rights in states were local and state authorities kept blacks from registering and voting. The act made the central government the voting registrar for potential black voters.

   These acts and other legislation have been extremely effective. Racial segregation in public accommodations has been virtually eliminated in the South, and the number of black voters has increased impressively. The nature of politics in the South has begun to change as a result, and the votes of southern blacks helped Georgia's Jimmy Carter to carry most of the South in the 1976 presidential election.

6. *The Gulf of Tonkin* is located between the Vietnamese mainland and the island of Hainan off the south coast of China. The Gulf of Tonkin has given its name to the Gulf of Tonkin Resolution adopted by Congress in August 1964. The Resolution authorized the president to "take all necessary measures to repel any armed attack against the forces of the United States" and to use military force to assist any member of the Southeast Asia Collective Defense Treaty who requested help "in defense of freedom."

   The Resolution was passed at President Johnson's request after a report that North Vietnamese torpedo boats had attacked U.S. Navy vessels in the Gulf of Tonkin. Although there was at the time some question as to the accuracy of the reports, Congress adopted the Resolution. It later became clear that the original ship attack report was, to say the least, misleading. In any case, President Johnson used the Gulf of Tonkin Resolution as a legalization of the expanding military role of the United States in Vietnam. Some members of Congress later complained that they had been misled by the administration about the events that sparked the Resolution.

Self-Test

I. Match each identifying statement with the appropriate name.

   a. John Foster Dulles (886)   e. Eugene McCarthy (907)
   b. Earl Warren (893)   f. Neil Armstrong (882)
   c. Orval Faubus (894–895)   g. Richard Nixon (890)
   d. Barry Goldwater (893)   h. Dean Rusk

1. _____ A conservative Republican, he was perceived by many as an extremist when he campaigned for the presidency against President Johnson in 1964.

2. _____ The American space program reached its climax when he became the first man to walk on the moon.

3. _____ As Chief Justice, he spoke for a unanimous Supreme Court in the historic decision which held that racial segregation in public schools was unconstitutional.

4. _____ His surprising popularity in the early Democratic primaries in 1968 forced President Johnson to reconsider his plans to run for reelection.

5. _____ President Eisenhower's rigidly anticommunist secretary of state who associated his name with the art of what he called "brinksmanship" diplomacy.

II. Circle the phrase that best completes each statement.

1. The public's admiration of the astronauts and the space program indicated its great confidence in the value of   (a) mass consumerism, (b) massed expertise,   (c) mass production. (882)

2. One domestic consequence of the Cold War and containment was that   (a) a military-industrial complex was able to determine national policy,   (b) much of the American public became disinterested in foreign policy problems,   (c) military expenditures now dominated the peacetime budget. (885)

3. In the 1950s and 1960s, American foreign policy was steadfastly opposed to   (a) revolution,   (b) the liberation of subject peoples, (c) the status quo. (888)

4. The Supreme Court ruled that public schools must be desegregated in   (a) *Brown* v. *Board of Education,*   (b) *Plessy* v. *Ferguson,* (c) the *Miranda* case. (893)

5. Martin Luther King, Jr.,'s strategy against the segregationists involved the use of   (a) peaceful compromise,   (b) violent confrontation, (c) mass resistance. (895)

6. America's involvement in Vietnam was based upon   (a) the central assumption of the containment policy,   (b) ignorance of the facts, miscalculation, and accident,   (c) treaty obligations to use military force. (900–901)

7. Domestic skepticism and opposition to the war in Vietnam spread

261

rapidly following the   (a) Gulf of Tonkin incident,   (b) commencement of aerial bombing, in North Vietnam   (c) Tet Offensive. (902)

8. One of the more important results of the Vietnam War was that it (a) accelerated the decline of containment policy,   (b) prevented the spread of communist Chinese influence into Southeast Asia, (c) prevented the North Vietnamese from taking over South Vietnam. (903)

9. The most lasting outgrowth of the rebellious movements of the 1960s was the   (a) free speech movement,   (b) women's rights movement,   (c) peace movement. (906)

Answers to the Self-Test

I. 1. d; 2. f; 3. b; 4. e; 5. a
II. 1. b; 2. c; 3. a; 4. a; 5. c; 6. a; 7. c; 8. a; 9. b

CHAPTER 33

An Elusive Stability

The Historical Problem

The final problem is to explain how Americans resolved the bitter social and political conflicts that had exploded in the 1960s. How did conflict and suspicion influence politics and the political process? How did national political leaders react to this social conflict? What domestic and foreign policies did the Nixon administration adopt? What effect did those policies have on the conflicts within American society? How did those policies influence the modernization of American life? What is the relationship between the policies of Presidents Ford and Carter and those of Nixon?

The Historical Problem Answered: The Chapter Thesis

The social conflict and political confusion apparent at the time of the 1968 presidential election forced political leaders to take into account the actual divisions within American society in order to form some of the groups into a coalition.

Richard Nixon succeeded in broadening the base of his political support after winning the presidency in 1968. As president, Nixon moved to redress the balance of power between national authority and localities and to calm local anxieties about national intervention. His appointments to the Supreme Court reduced the Court's inclination to expand the authority of the central government. The new national policy balance of the 1970s involved a number of cautious accommodations between minority rights and local cultural autonomy. This new balance between nationalism and localism accounted for Nixon's 1972 reelection. And Nixon's presidential successors have followed the path he marked.

In Vietnam, the Nixon administration reduced domestic opposition to the war by increasing the application of military power while gradually withdrawing American troops. The agreement reached in January 1973 allowed the war to continue without American soldiers. The Nixon-Kissinger foreign policy countered the erosion of containment by improving relations with communist China and by moving toward détente with Russia. Foreign policy also accepted the diversity of world nationalisms, which meant that the United States operated without a systematic foreign policy. But some of the Cold War assumptions — the necessity for a nuclear arsenal, for example — endured.

The economy began to falter and to suffer from inflation at the same time; worldwide inflation meant that the traditional techniques of fiscal management no longer worked. Most Americans seemed to agree with President Ford that control of inflation should take priority. But neither Ford nor his successor, Carter, was able to find a way to solve the double problem of inflation and recession.

During the 1970s, anxiety over the plight of the individual in the modern world increased as some successful Americans began to realize that they were not necessarily protected from the manipulative techniques they had assumed were applied only to others. In the fall from power of Vice-President Agnew and then of President Nixon, Americans discovered that no one was inviolable. In 1980, as public problems expanded in size and complexity, two conditions made the future more cloudy than usual. One was that the shrinkage of the central government's authority had diminished its ability to deal with these public problems. And the second was the disenchantment with the national system that was spreading throughout American society. The Great Republic awaited a new formulation of political methods and social purposes.

The Chain of Arguments and Evidence

People, Places, and Events

1. *Richard M. Nixon* (1913–   ) is one of the most enigmatic public men in American political history. Nixon was born in 1913 in California where he attended local schools and Whittier College before moving on to Duke University Law School in North Carolina. He received his law degree in 1937 in the midst of the Great Depression. Unable to join the Federal Bureau of Investigation, the young lawyer joined a law firm in Whittier, California. During the Second World War, he worked in the tire-rationing section of the Office of Price Administration, an experience which, by his own recollection, made him less confident about the possible effectiveness of government bureaucracy. He then joined the Navy and served from 1942 to 1946 as a commissioned officer.

   Returning from the service, Nixon ran for the House of Representatives in 1946 and was reelected in 1948. Nixon's 1946 election campaign is particularly significant because it centered on the campaign charge, partly explicit and partly by innuendo, that Nixon's Democratic opponent was un-American and perhaps tied to communism. In the House, Nixon was largely a regular Republican, and he was appointed to the House Un-American Activities Committee, a post which brought him to national attention. It was as a member of that committee that he became involved in the Alger Hiss case; Nixon believed Whittaker Chambers, an admitted former communist, when Chambers charged that Alger Hiss, a State Department official in the Roosevelt administration, had participated in espionage activities with Chambers. Nixon was one of the committee members who pushed the case against Hiss, which resulted in Hiss's conviction for perjury.

   Elected to the United States Senate in 1950, Nixon was then elected vice-president on the Republican ticket with Eisenhower in 1952 and 1956. Nixon was always a controversial figure in politics. His political positions generally were moderate Republican, but his highly partisan attacks on Democrats often included the charge that they were disloyal. Many people considered him the master of the political smear, a man whose main contribution to national politics was to lower its tone. But many Republicans saw him as a vigorous supporter of moderate Republican domestic policies, a strong defense, and an energetic foreign policy. Although he lacked personal warmth and the ability to relate easily to people, Nixon used the vice-presidency to make himself the national spokesman for the Republican party, a task made easier by the fact that President Eisenhower tried to stay above politics.

In 1960 Nixon inherited the Republican nomination from Eisenhower, but lost a very close election to John F. Kennedy. He then ran for the governorship of California in 1962 and was defeated again, a blow that prompted his retirement from politics. He joined a law firm in New York City where he engaged in a corporate law practice for the next few years.

His drive for the Republican party nomination in 1968 and his electoral victory in the national election is one of the great political comebacks in modern political history. Given Nixon's unorthodox career, it is perhaps not totally surprising that his impressive victories of 1968 and 1972 should have ended with the disgrace of his resignation and acceptance of a presidential pardon. Perhaps not even Nixon knows why the Watergate disaster enveloped his administration. It is possible, however, that in the excitement of the election campaign the president and his associates lapsed back into the "politics is war" and "anything goes" tactics that Nixon had used so successfully in political campaigns during the early days of the Cold War.

2. *Spiro T. Agnew* (1918–   ) was President Nixon's vice-president, and his resignation forecast the eventual fate of the whole administration. Agnew was born in Baltimore, Maryland, the son of Greek immigrants. He was educated at Johns Hopkins University and studied law at the University of Baltimore. In the late 1950s, Agnew involved himself in local Republican party politics in predominantly Democratic Maryland. He was elected to a county post and then, in 1966, to the governorship, a victory that depended partly on the support of reform Democrats.

Nixon surprised nearly everyone by selecting Agnew to be his running mate in 1968. This was widely interpreted as an implementation of the Republicans' southern strategy which was designed to win electoral votes in traditionally Democratic southern states. As vice-president, Agnew modeled himself on Nixon's vice-presidency, and he became the partisan spokesman for the Republican party and the public controversialist of the administration. This allowed President

Nixon to follow President Eisenhower's example and remain above the partisan political fight, at least part of the time. In this capacity, Agnew expressed the values of local America by attacking intellectuals, college students, and the news media.

The man who made himself the administration's voice of righteousness, ironically, was discovered to have been guilty of accepting bribes, and he made the equivalent of a guilty plea to avoid a trial on a more serious charge. His resignation signaled the beginning of the end of the Nixon administration.

3. *Watergate* is actually a very large apartment and office complex located in Washington, D.C. Because the national headquarters of the Democratic party was burglarized there, the name of the apartment-office complex has been attached to the whole affair. Disaster resulted when the Nixon administration attempted to conceal its involvement in the burglary and the financial irregularities that occurred in the campaign.

4. *George C. Wallace* (1919–   ) is a former governor of Alabama and a regional political leader who has influenced national politics. Wallace was born and educated in Alabama where he received a law degree from the University of Alabama in 1942. He served in the Second World War, then took up the practice of law. He was elected a state district judge in 1952, but was defeated when he ran for the governorship in 1958.

In 1962, he ran again and was elected. National attention followed his flamboyant public opposition to racial integration in Alabama. He developed a regional following in the South by speaking out vigorously against civil rights legislation and federally-imposed racial desegregation, and in favor of states' rights, white supremacy, and local autonomy. His admirers saw Wallace as a populist defender of the interests of working-class and lower middle-class Americans everywhere who were ignored by the central government. Critics saw Wallace as a demagogue who ignored the real problems of his state and the nation in order to maintain his own political power by making race an issue.

Wallace ran in the Democratic state primaries in 1964 as a presidential candidate; in 1968 he broke with the Democratic party to run as the candidate of the American Independent party, but his appeal was largely regional. Wallace campaigned again in 1972 for the Democratic nomination, but his tone had changed partly, no doubt, because of the political effects of the Voting Rights Act of 1965, which had increased the number of black voters in the South. Wallace's appeal to the ignored little man was still strong, but the racial content of his campaign was considerably diminished.

An assassination attempt during the primary campaign left him paralyzed from the waist down. He gamely tried to continue the race, but his body was not as tough as his will. The primary victories in the South by Jimmy Carter, and Carter's national victory in 1976 suggested that a new political day had dawned in the South, a day in which politics would not be based on race.

Self-Test

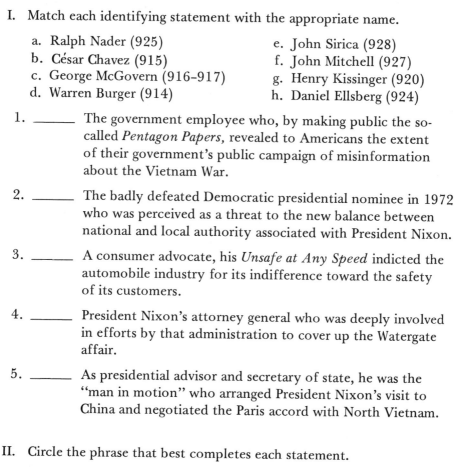

I. Match each identifying statement with the appropriate name.

a. Ralph Nader (925)   e. John Sirica (928)
b. César Chavez (915)   f. John Mitchell (927)
c. George McGovern (916–917)   g. Henry Kissinger (920)
d. Warren Burger (914)   h. Daniel Ellsberg (924)

1. _____ The government employee who, by making public the so-called *Pentagon Papers,* revealed to Americans the extent of their government's public campaign of misinformation about the Vietnam War.

2. _____ The badly defeated Democratic presidential nominee in 1972 who was perceived as a threat to the new balance between national and local authority associated with President Nixon.

3. _____ A consumer advocate, his *Unsafe at Any Speed* indicted the automobile industry for its indifference toward the safety of its customers.

4. _____ President Nixon's attorney general who was deeply involved in efforts by that administration to cover up the Watergate affair.

5. _____ As presidential advisor and secretary of state, he was the "man in motion" who arranged President Nixon's visit to China and negotiated the Paris accord with North Vietnam.

II. Circle the phrase that best completes each statement.

1. President Nixon began the withdrawal of American troops from Vietnam as a part of a strategy to   (a) win the war,   (b) quiet antiwar protests at home,   (c) save money. (917)

2. President Nixon's policy toward the Soviet Union was one of (a) détente,   (b) containment,   (c) isolationism. (918)

3. Most Americans perceived their most important problem in the late

1970s to be related to   (a) international peace,   (b) race relations,   (c) the economy. (923)

4. President Nixon resigned from office because he   (a) had failed to
find a solution to the Vietnam War,   (b) was embarrassed by the
criminal misconduct and resignation of his vice-president, Spiro Agnew,
(c) was found to be involved in the cover-up of the Watergate affair.
(928)

5. Both Presidents Ford and Carter were noted for their   (a) honesty,
(b) inspirational leadership,   (c) close working relationship with
Congress. (929)

Answers to the Self-Test

I. 1. h; 2. c; 3. a; 4. f; 5. g
II. 1. b; 2. a; 3. c; 4. c; 5. a

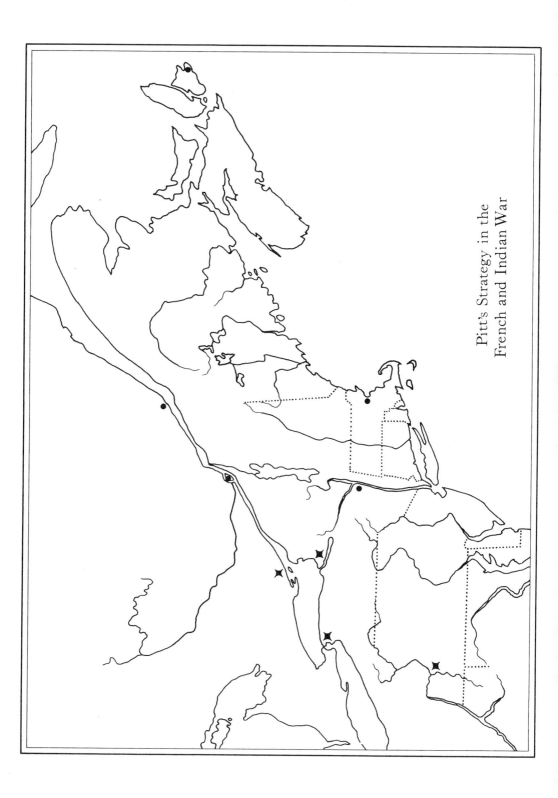

Pitt's Strategy in the
French and Indian War

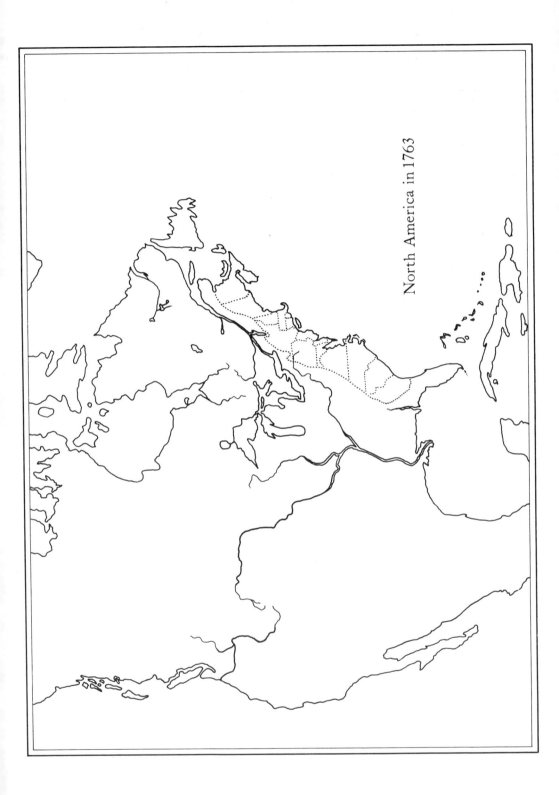

North America in 1763

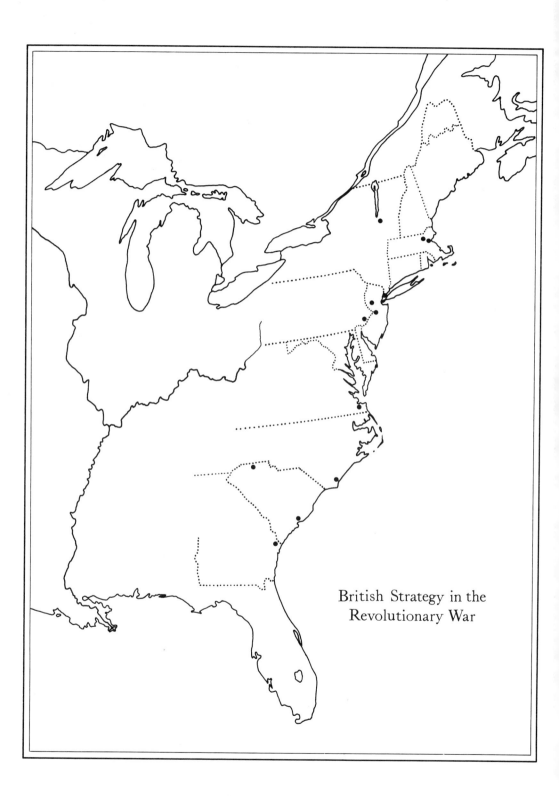

British Strategy in the
Revolutionary War

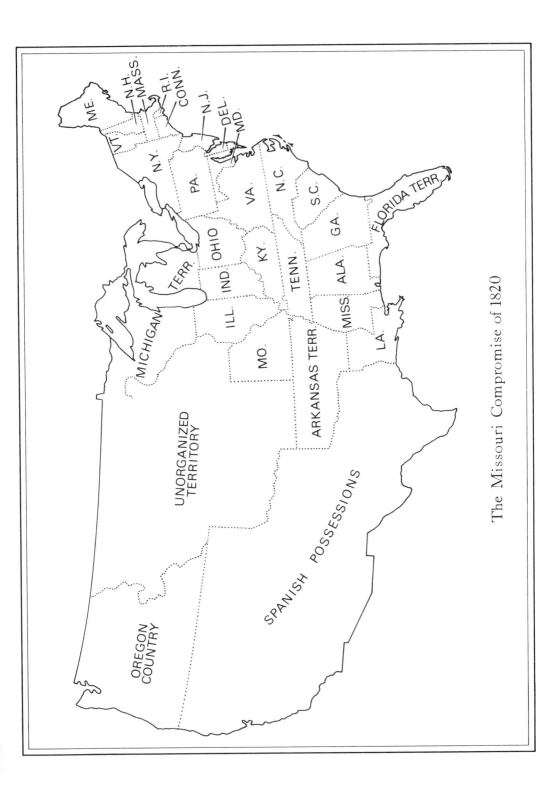

The Missouri Compromise of 1820

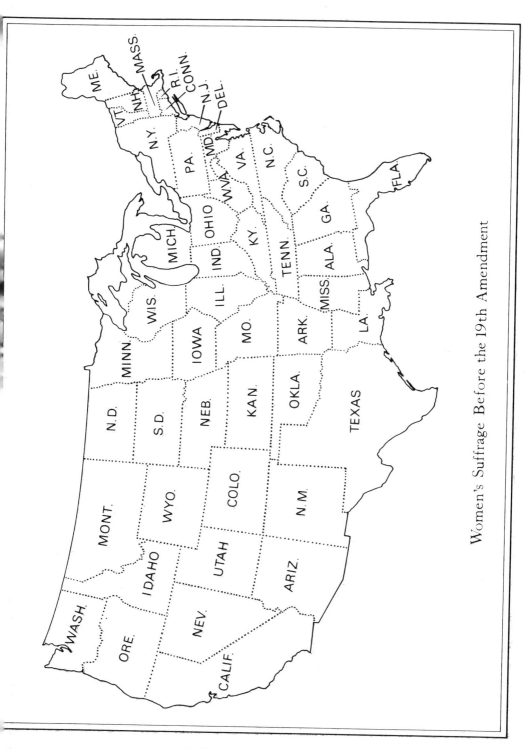

Women's Suffrage Before the 19th Amendment

1 2 3 4 5 6 7 8 9 0

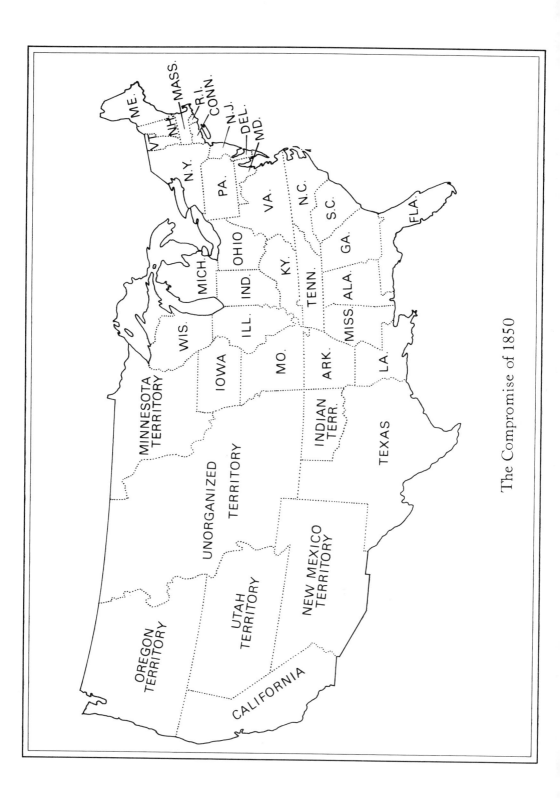

The Compromise of 1850

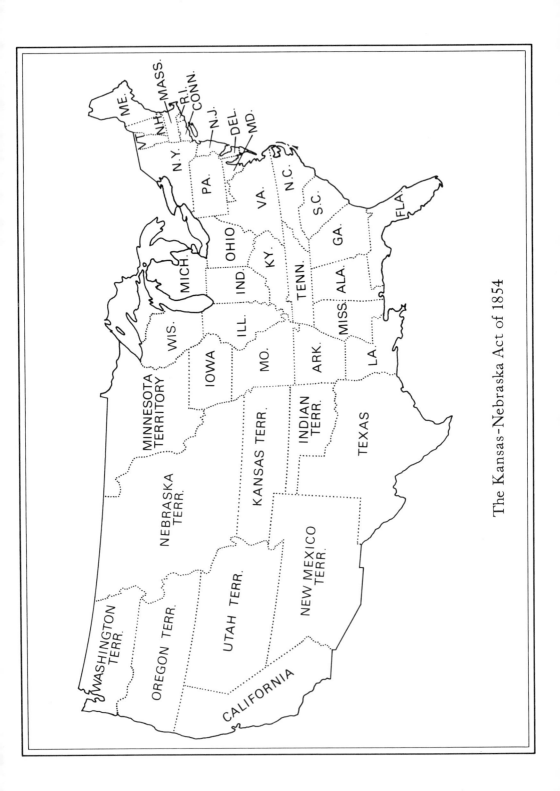

The Kansas-Nebraska Act of 1854

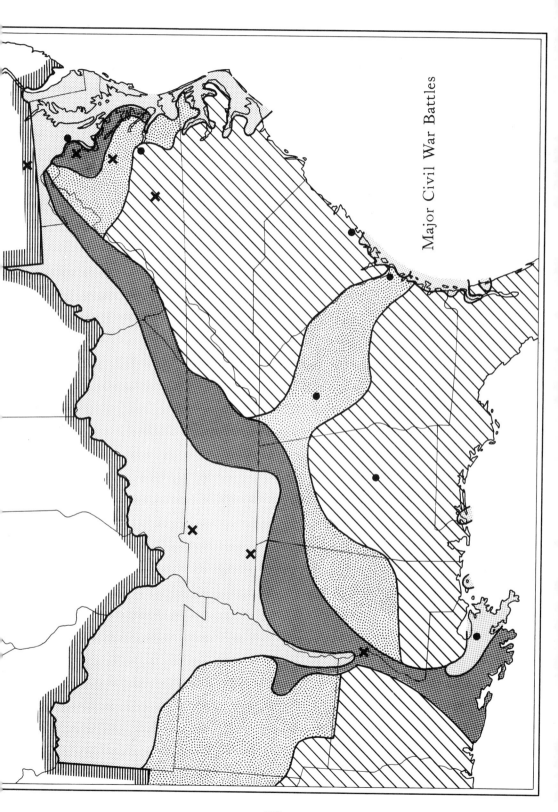

Major Civil War Battles

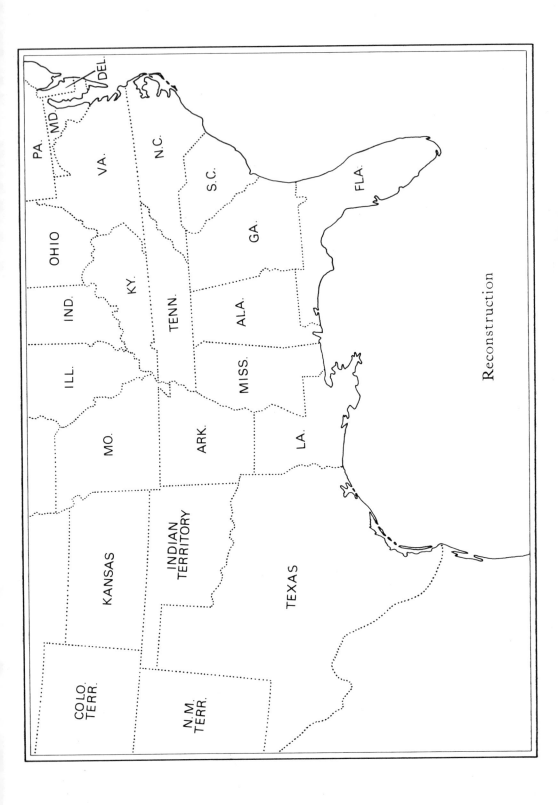

Reconstruction